RANDOLF JIMENEZ

THE GROOVE SCHOOLBOOK

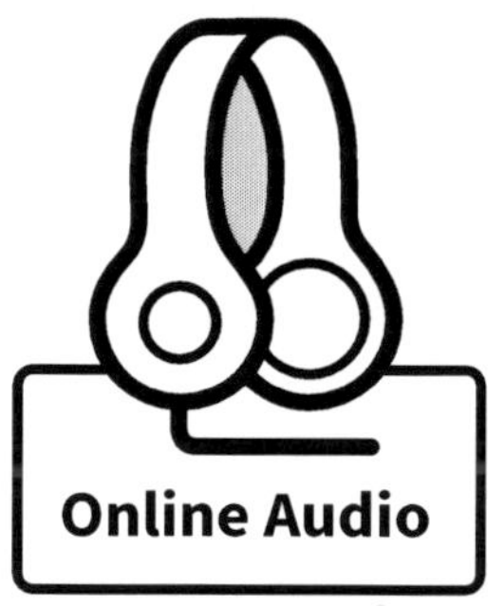

To access the online audio go to:
WWW.MELBAY.COM/30974MEB

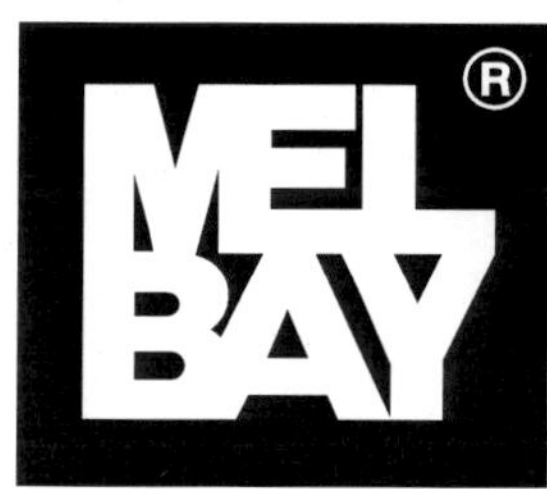

WWW.MELBAY.COM

DEDICATION

To the loving memory of my brother, **Harold Jimenez**, whose words of motivation
are a daily source of inspiration in my mind and my being.
I am eternally grateful for having had the opportunity of growing up with
him, and deeply knowing such a wonderful human being.

AKNOWLEDGEMENTS

To God for giving me life, energy, time and opportunity to teach and pass on my knowledge. All glory to Him.

To my wife for all her unconditional love and support, for being my greatest inspiration and motivation, for believing in me from day one. Nothing would be possible without her.

To my parents for their boundless love, and for teaching me the importance of discipline, honesty and perseverance.

To my siblings and brother-in-law for their constant support and encouragement.

To guitarist Ardenys Pimentel for his selfless support, time, energy, creativity and dedication in making this book a reality.

To all my students around the world for being a source of inspiration in my continued growth as a musician and teacher.

To the music industry manufacturers and their artist relationship representatives who have believed in me and given their support: Sonor, Paiste, Vater, Humes and Berg, and Audix.

To all the artists, musicians, producers and recording engineers with whom I have had the opportunity to work and learn.

To all the people who in one way or another have supported my career.

ABOUT THE AUTHOR

Accomplished drummer, percussionist, composer and educator, Randolf Jimenez, was born in Caracas, Venezuela. He first fell in love with drums at the age of 4 when his parents gave him a toy drum set as a Christmas present. He later began practicing drums on his own and by the age of 16, was already playing professionally in the Venezuelan music scene.

Randolf is a sound innovator with a passion for pushing creative boundaries. He is the kind of drummer who knows how to rock, vibe, swing, or relax into a minimalistic drum part when required. As a band leader, he has produced *Randolf Jimenez: Latin Jazz Project* and the rock fusion album, *MalosAires Trio* which was recorded in Buenos Aires. His recordings are distributed on all digital platforms.

His work has been featured on websites, newspapers and magazines in Venezuela, Europe, Japan, and Canada including *Billboard Magazine, All About Jazz, Malta Core, Drum Fills Kafé, Acid Conga, Tokyo Jazz Review, Latinos Magazine, Ultimas Noticias, A UNO Magazine, CARAS Magazine* and many others. Billboard Magazine named him "one of today's greatest Latin American drummers." He has also appeared on several TV shows in Venezuela, NET TV (Europe), Rogers TV Univision Canada and Univision Miami.

Randolf's style, impeccable timing and solid technique have not only earned him the respect of his fellow musicians, but also the title "The Groove" in the Venezuelan music community.

Since moving to Canada, Randolf has risen to the top of the Toronto music scene. His musicianship, versatility and professionalism keep him very busy with a wide variety of bands and *Grammy Award*-winning musicians and has rapidly become the most sought-after Latin drummer in Toronto. He has also toured extensively with his own band.

Randolf stays active in education by teaching an average of 45 students per week in the Toronto area. He has taught hundreds of students in both local music academies and international workshops.

Randolf Jimenez proudly endorses Sonor Drums, Paiste Cymbals, Vater Drumsticks, Humes & Berg Cases and Audix Microphones.

INTRODUCTION

The Groove Schoolbook was created to be a drum method used by students who want to learn the most common and popular rhythms for drumming. This method will help you to develop a strong rhythmic concept known as "groove".

Groove is a feeling, a sensation. It is a specific way to play where the rhythm feels tight and very precise. Groove can be achieved over time through deliberate practice and repetition of certain rhythmic patterns.

Many of the best drummers in the world are true groove masters. Some of them have achieved extremely successful careers due to their technique and understanding of a very precise sense of rhythm. That said, it is extremely important for the modern drummer to spend great amounts of time developing a solid groove.

In order to properly perform the coordination and independence exercises found in this method, I suggest finding a good teacher. The use of a metronome on a daily basis is also highly recommended as part of your practice routine.

It is my deep and sincere wish that this drum method contributes to the achievement of all your musical goals.

HOW TO USE THIS BOOK

1.- Practice the rhythm patterns as many times as needed at different speeds, until you can play consistently and without mistakes.

2.- Practice all the patterns from Part 1 playing the snare drum in the middle of the drumhead and then as rimshots.

3.- Practice all the patterns playing the hi-hat with the dominant hand and then, switch to the weak hand in order to develop ambidexterity.

4.- Once you finish Part 1 and Part 2, practice everything again, this time using the ride/ hi-hat, open hi-hat and sixteenth-note combinations from Part 3.

5.- Practice all exercises heel-down and then heel-up on the bass drum pedal in order to develop the ability to play at different dynamic levels.

6.- Practice all exercises from Part 5 again, this time playing the cymbal part on the ride and adding quarter notes to the hi-hat played with the foot.

DRUMSET NOTATION KEY

a. Bass drum
b. Snare drum
c. Hi-hat with foot
d. Hi-hat
e. Open Hi-hat
f. Ride cymbal

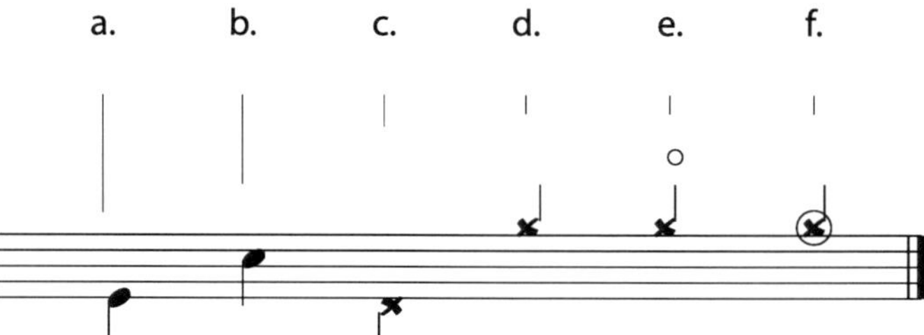

TABLE OF CONTENTS

PART 1

EIGHTH-NOTE GROOVES

AUDIO TRACKS

EIGHTH-NOTE GROOVES

PART 1

♩ =120

1

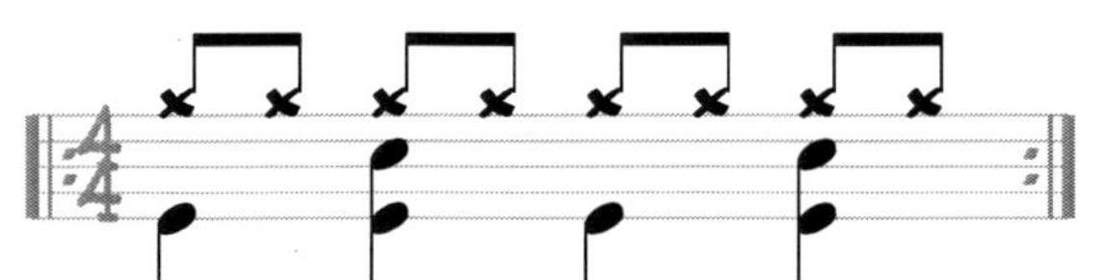

2

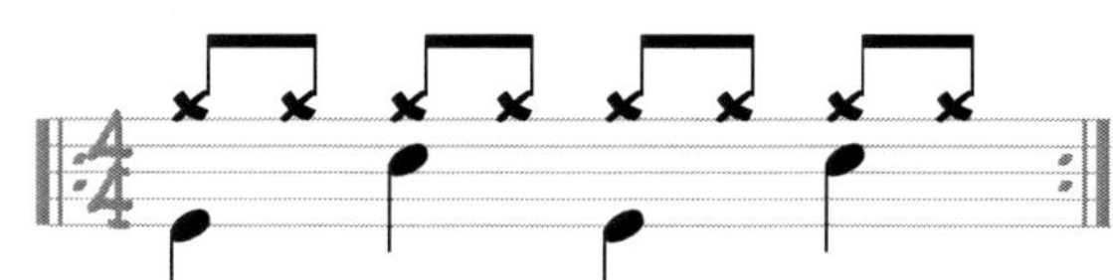

3

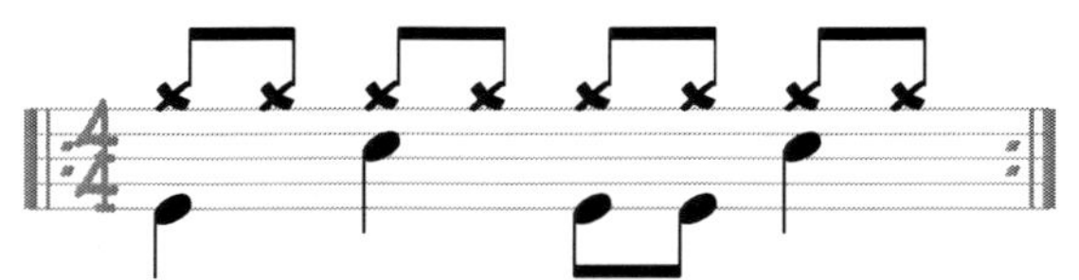

4

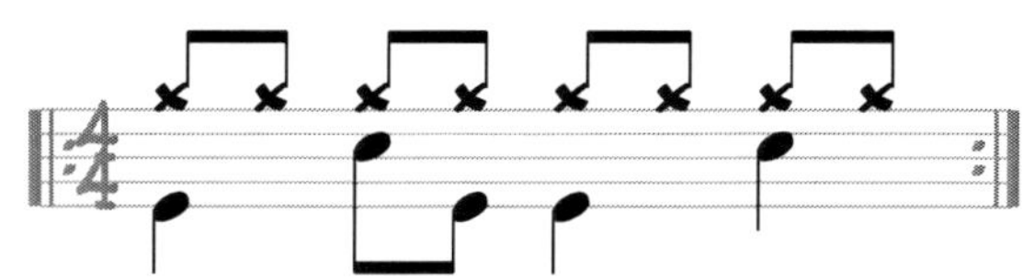

5

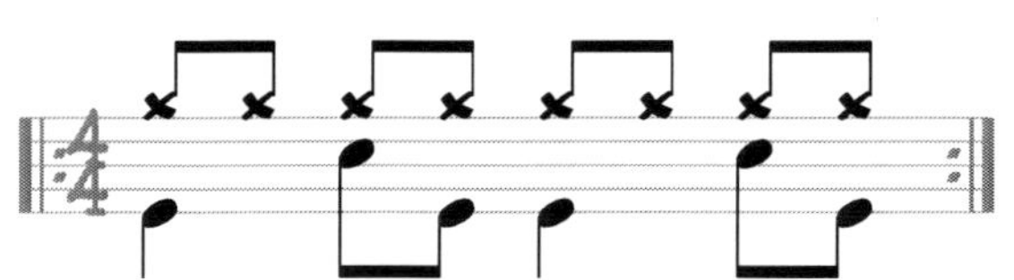

6

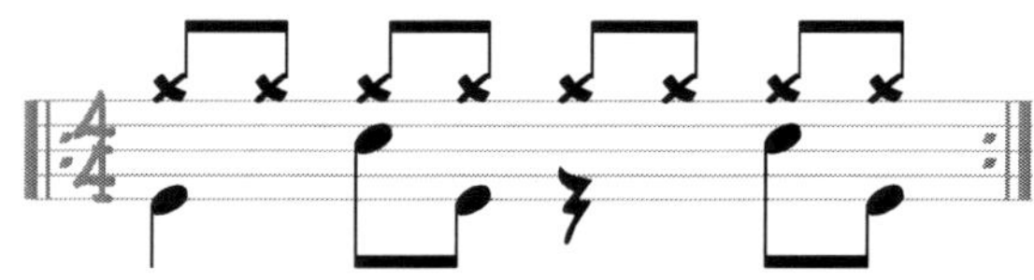

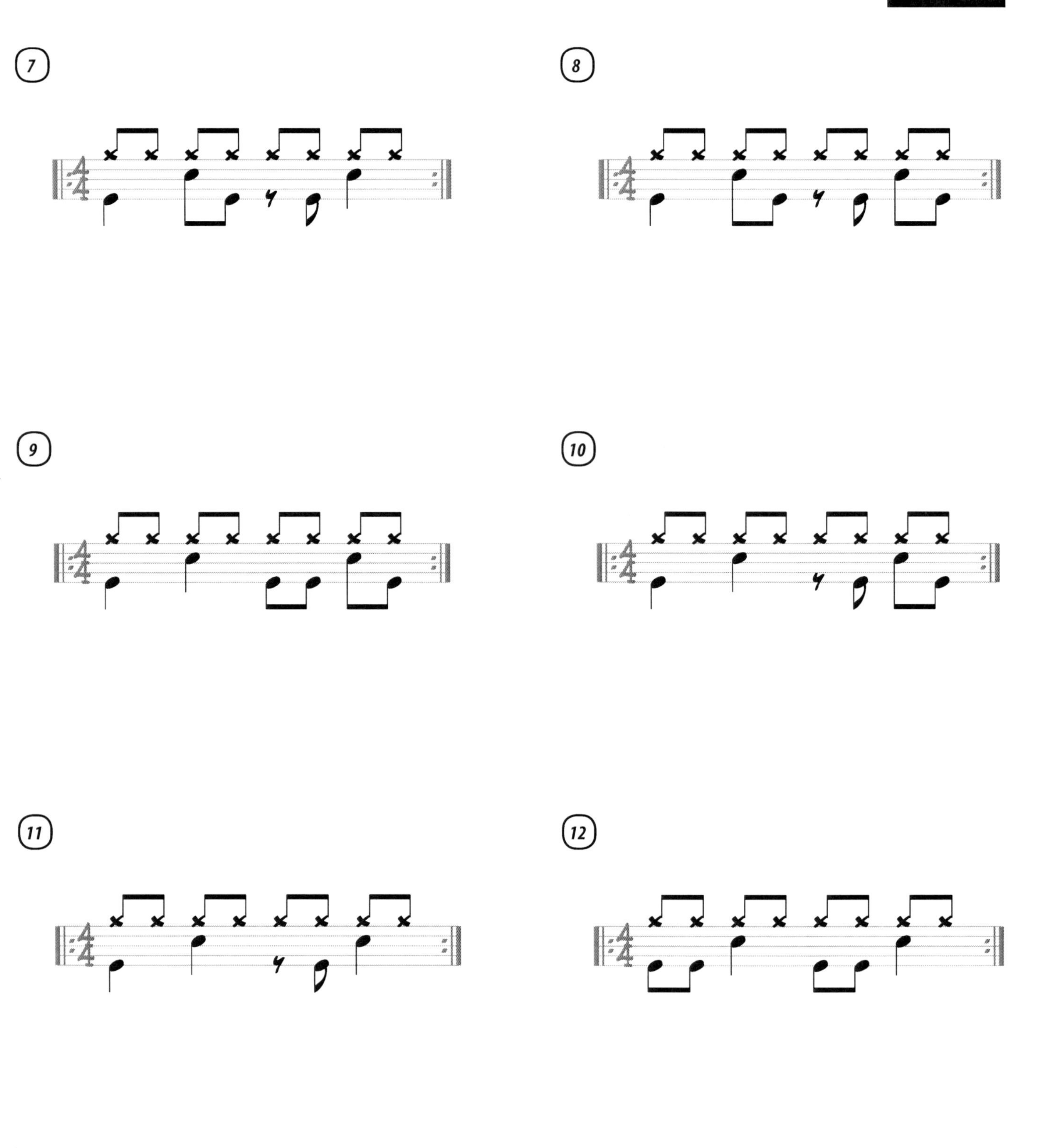
7
8
9
10
11
12

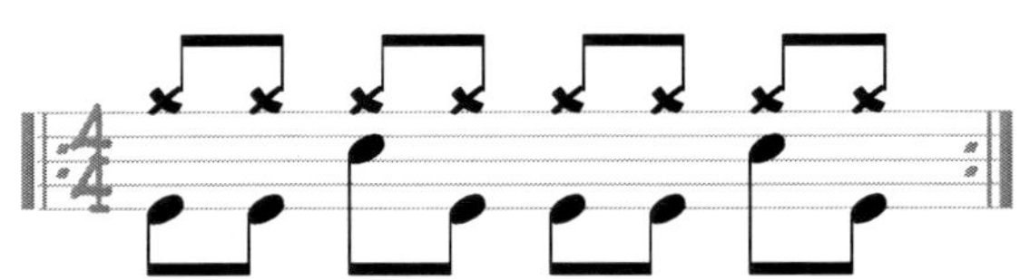

14

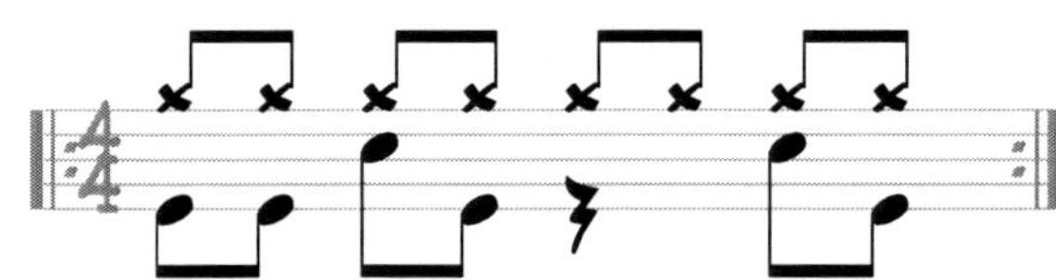

15

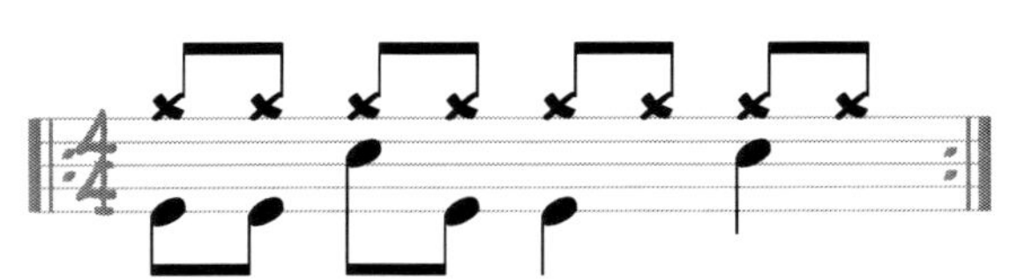

16

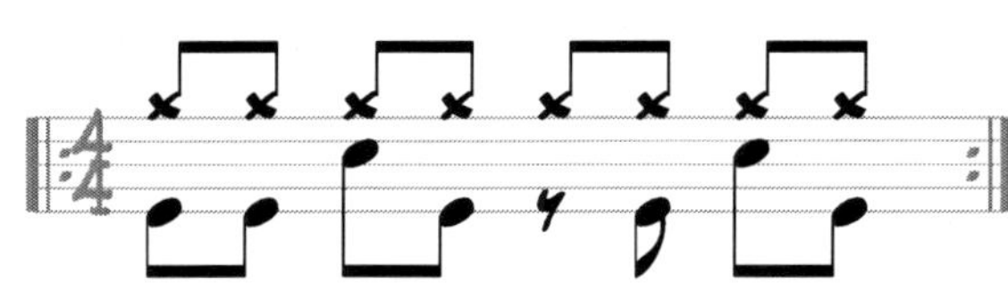

17

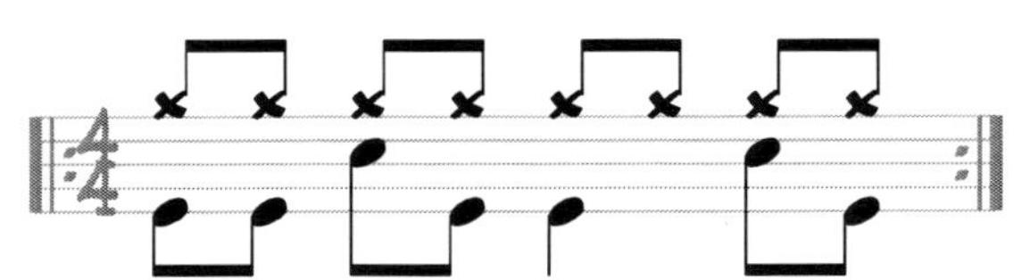

18

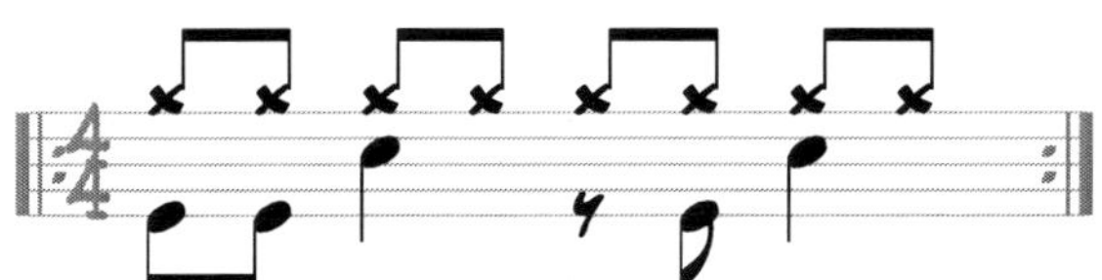

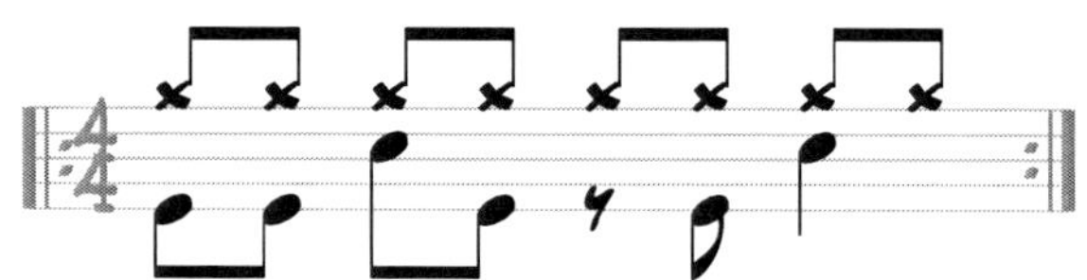

20

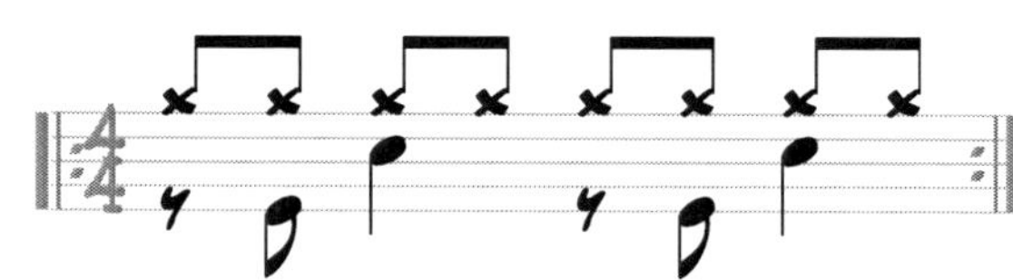

21

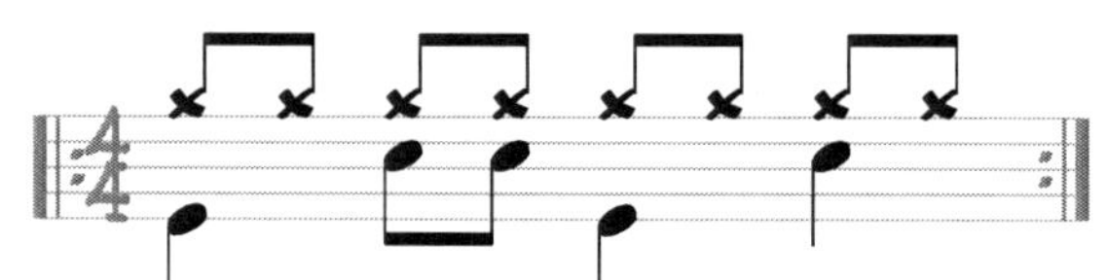

22

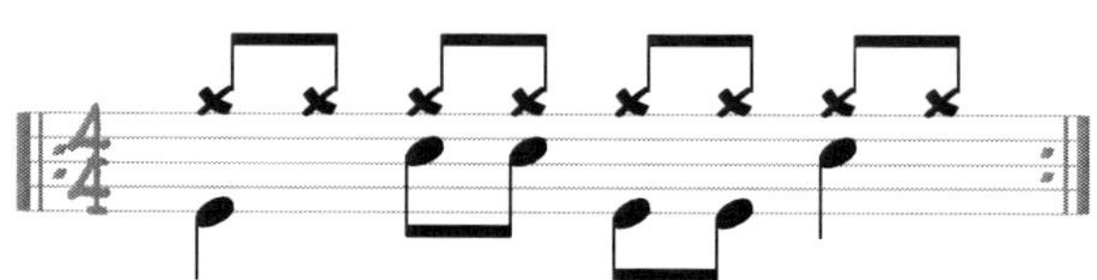

23

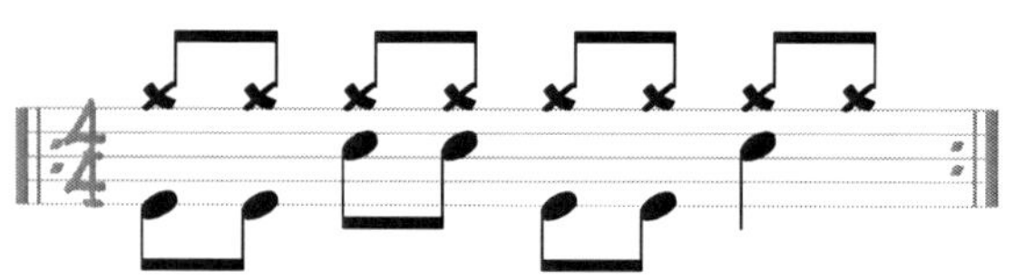

24

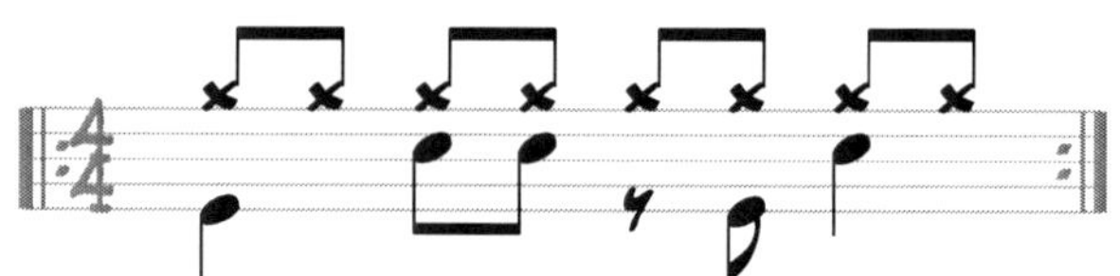

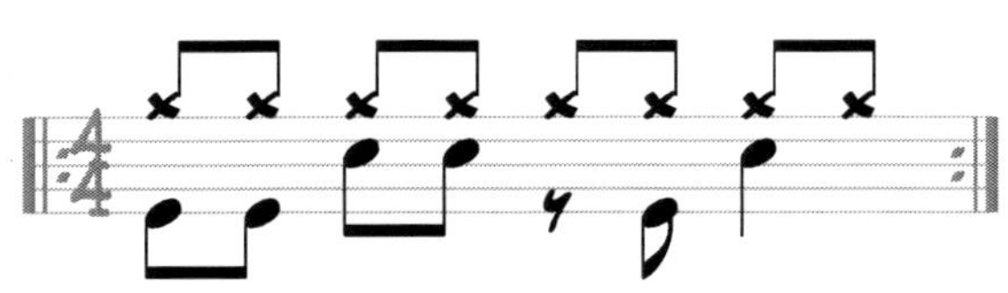

26

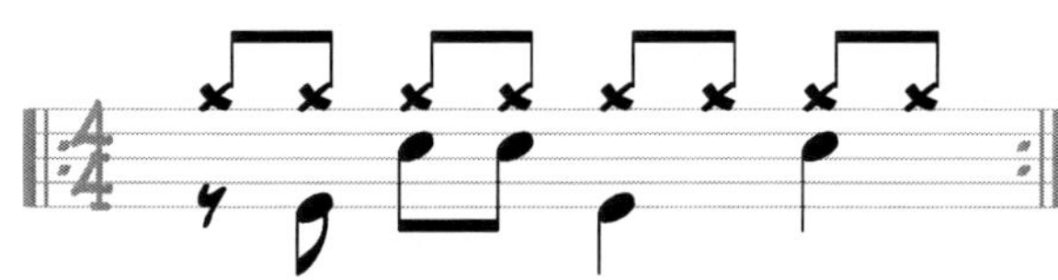

27

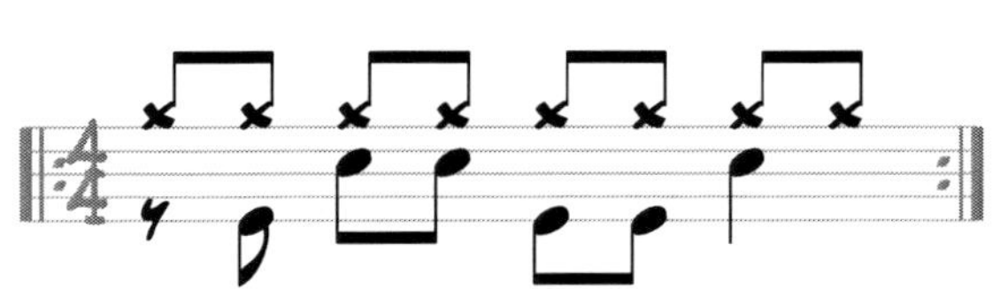

28

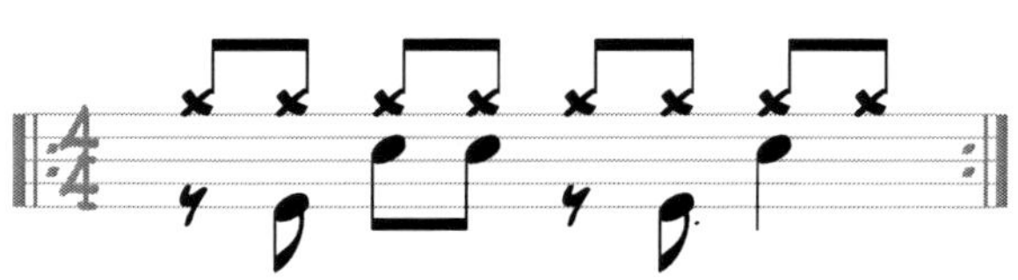

29

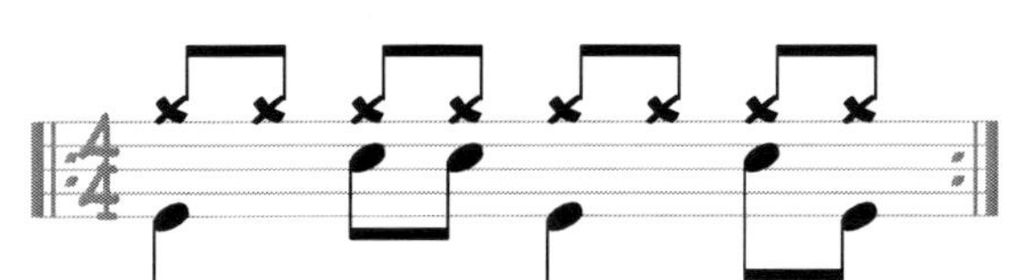

30

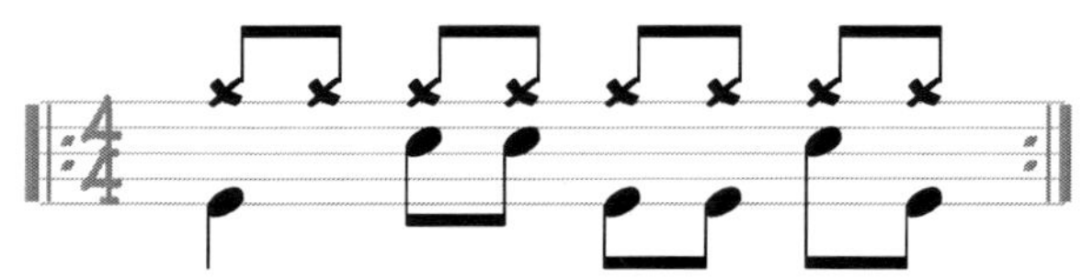

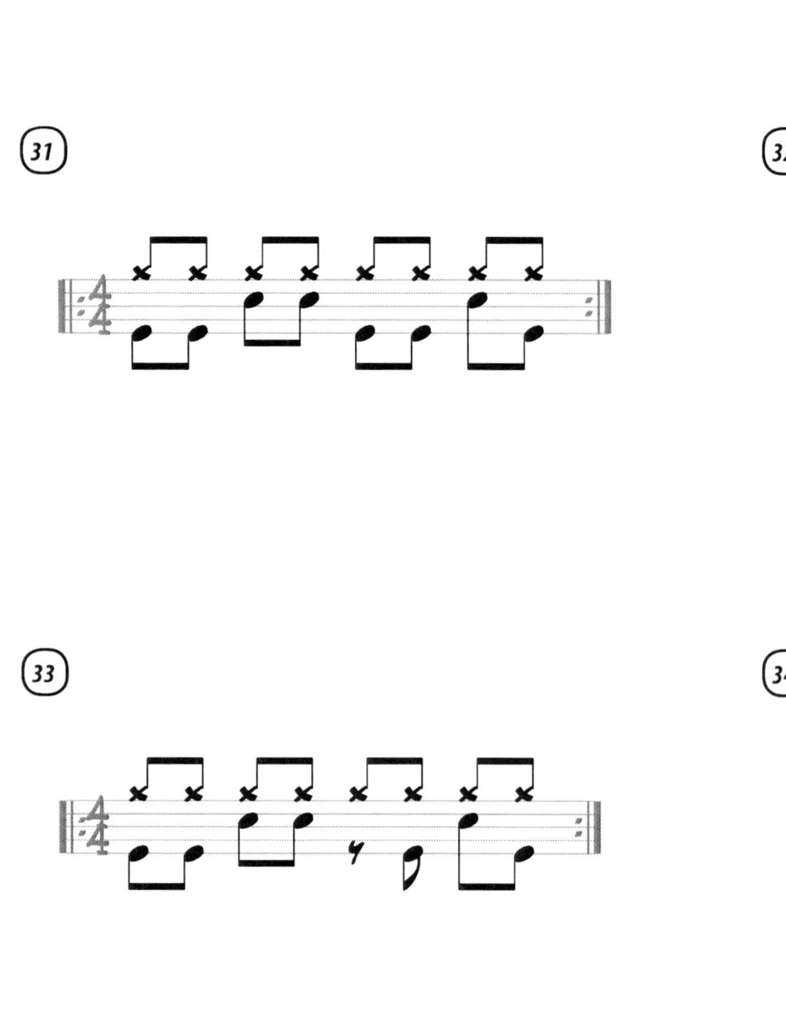

31

32

33

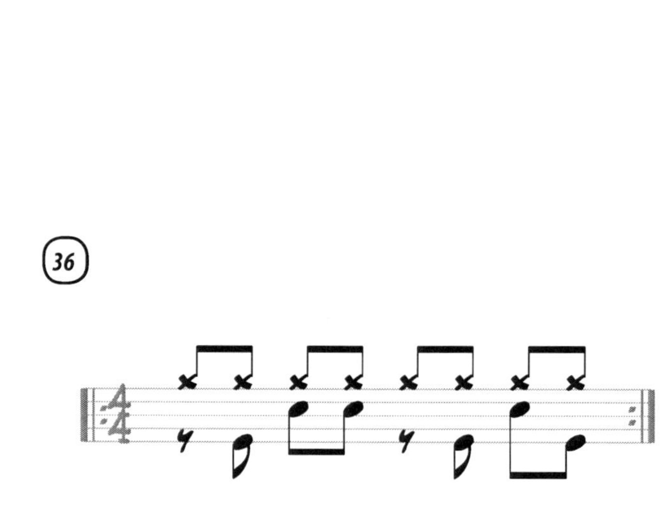

34

35

36

37

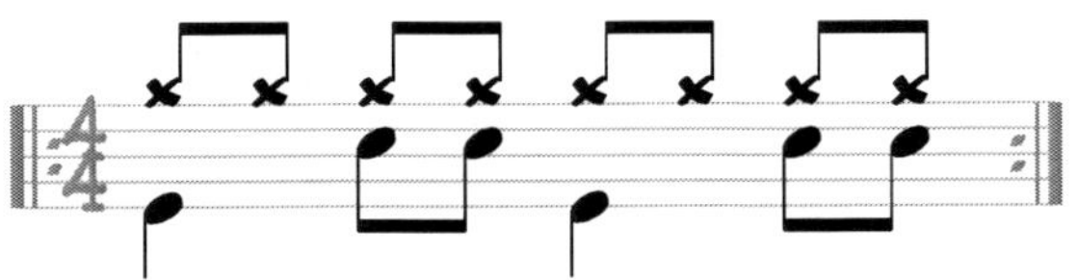

38

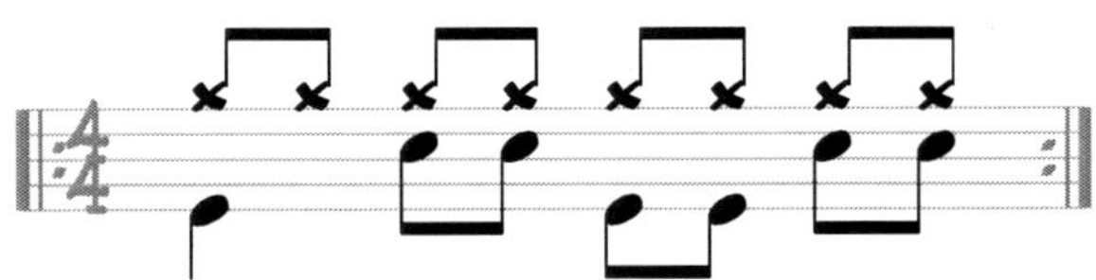

39

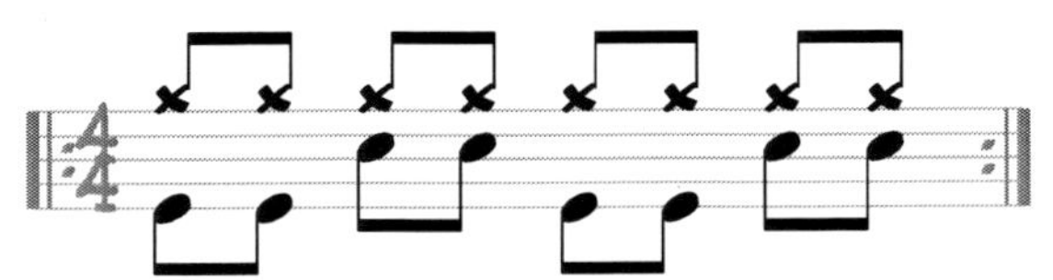

40

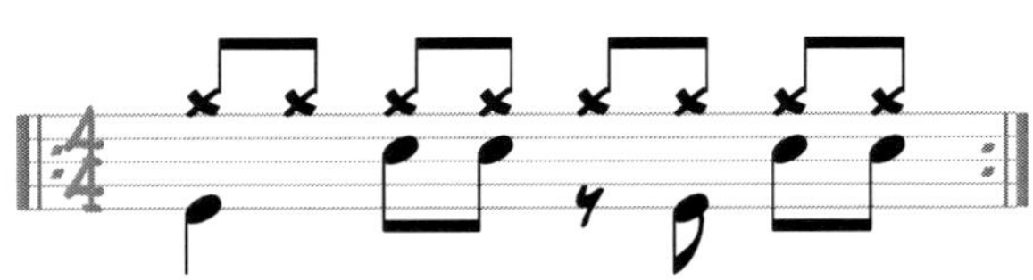

41

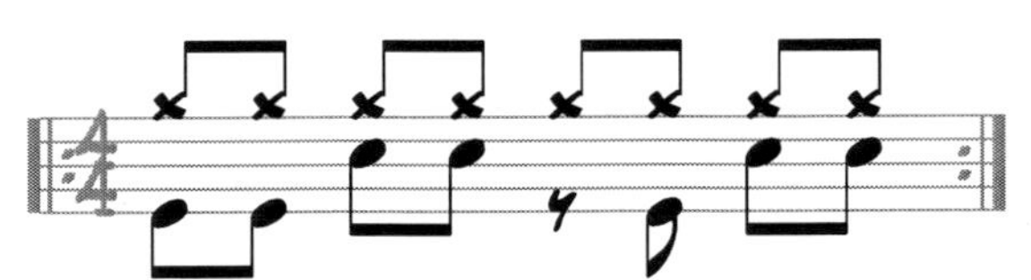

42

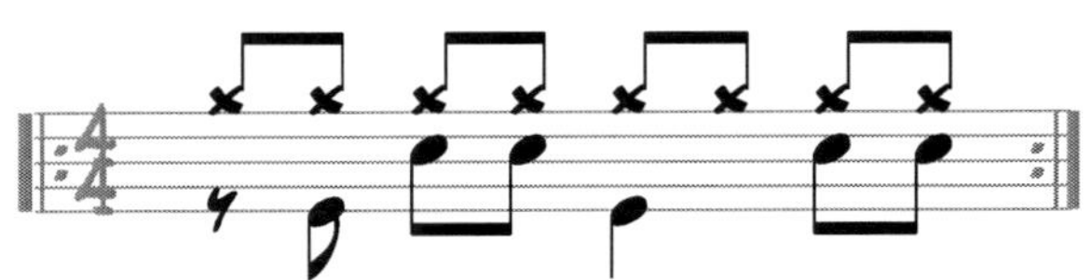

43

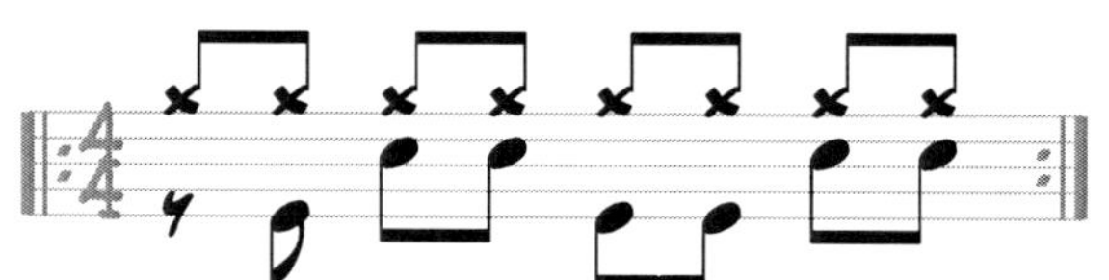

44

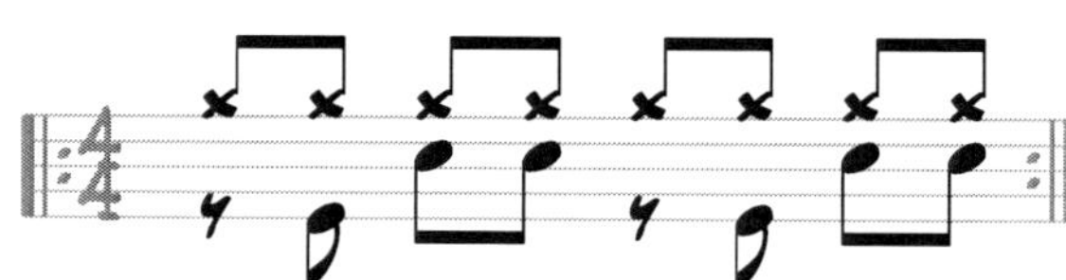

PART 2

SIXTEENTH-NOTE GROOVES

AUDIO TRACKS

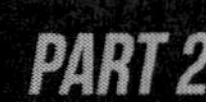

♩ =120

(1)

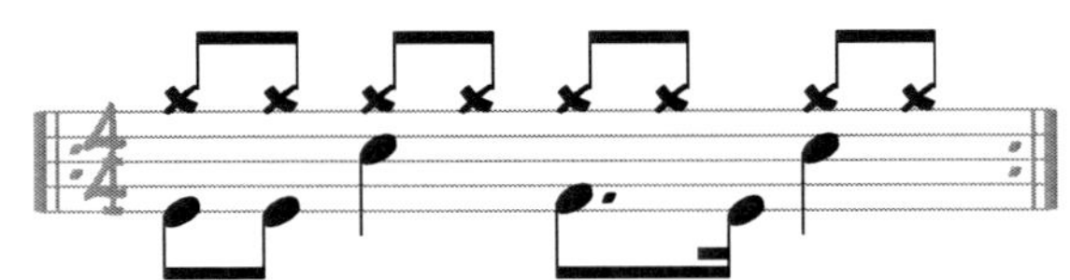

(2)

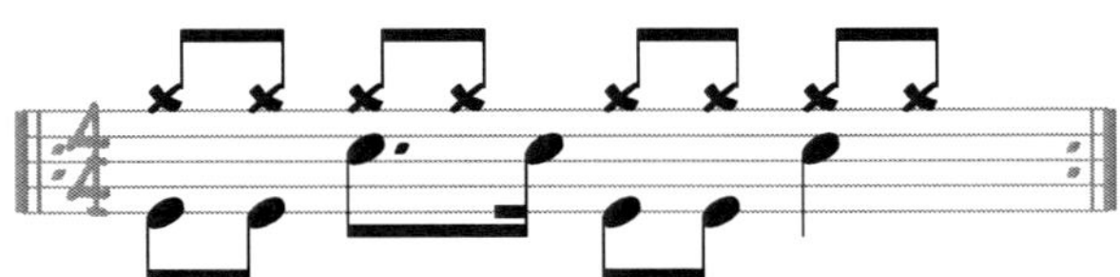

(3)

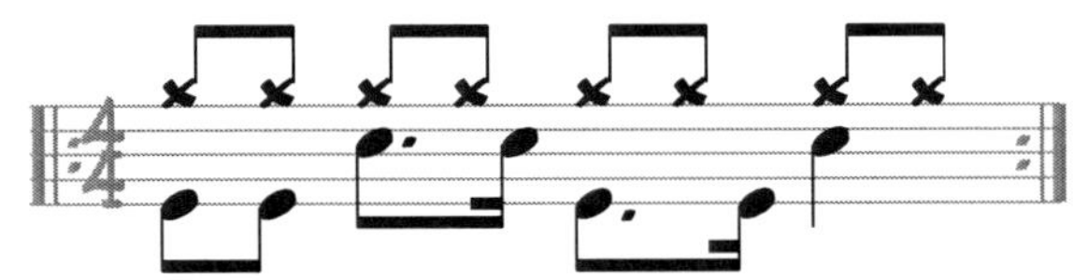

(4)

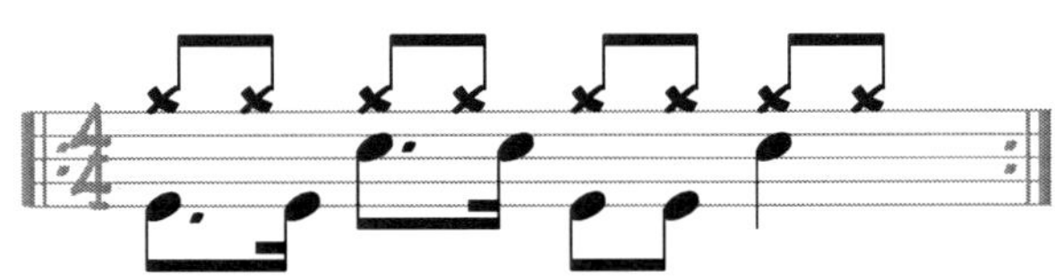

(5)

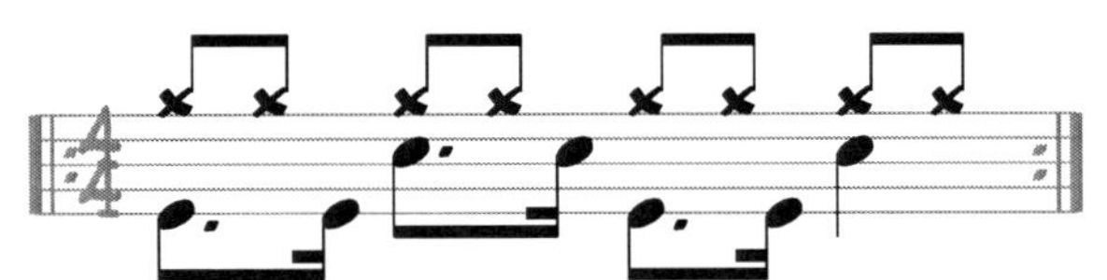

(6)

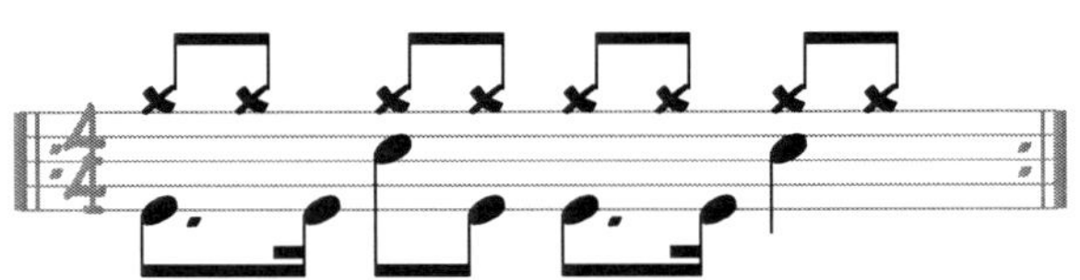

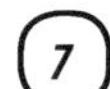

(7)

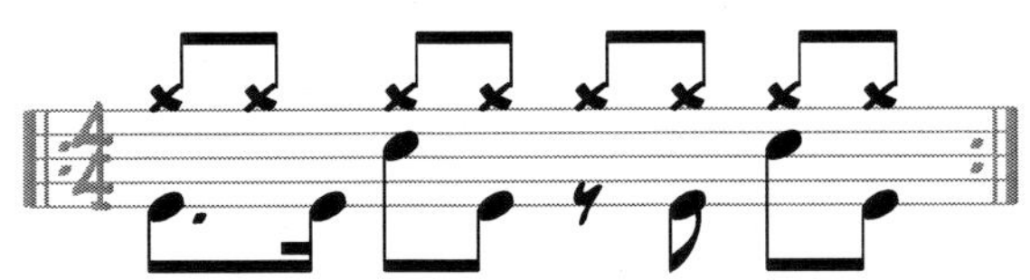

(8)

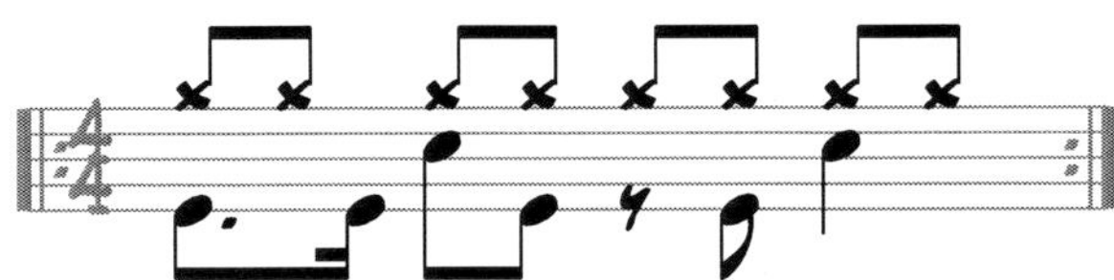

(9)

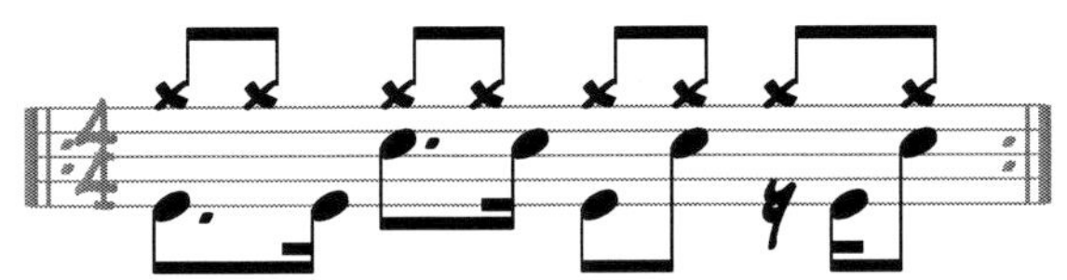

(10)

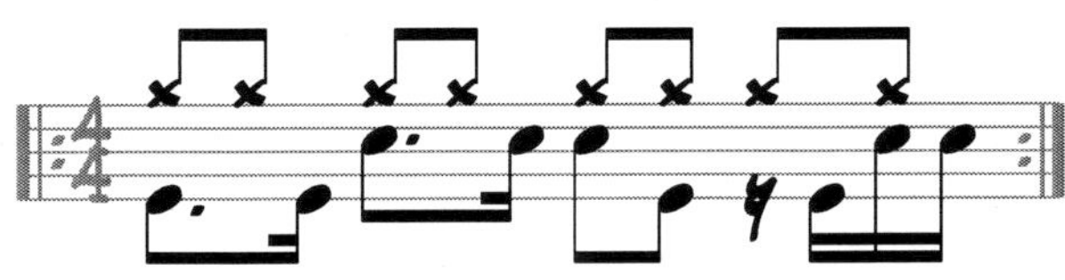

(11)

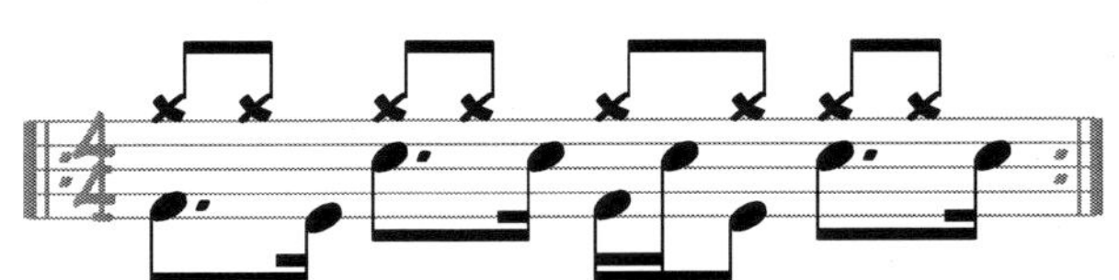

(12)

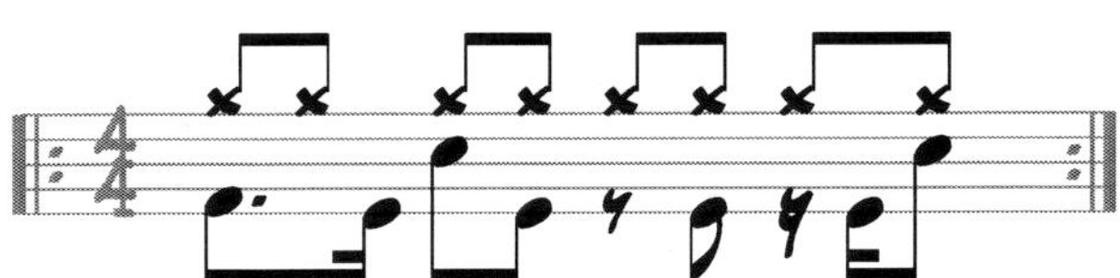

13

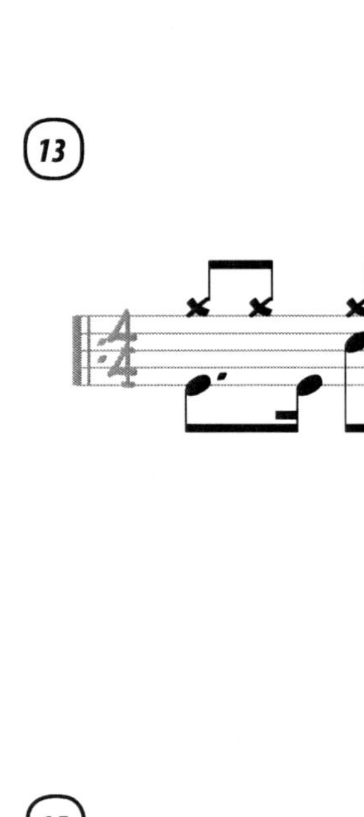

14

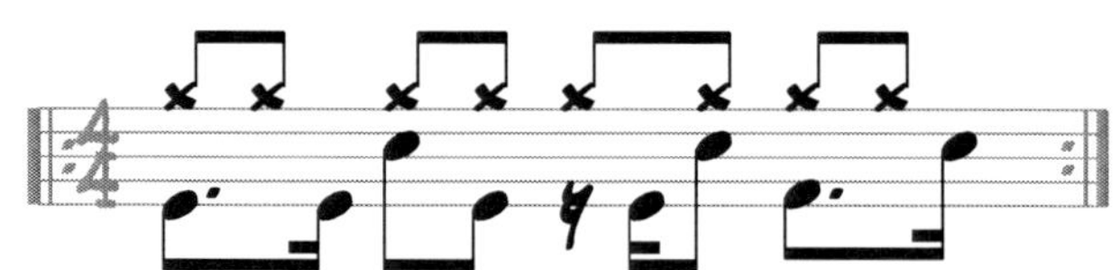

15

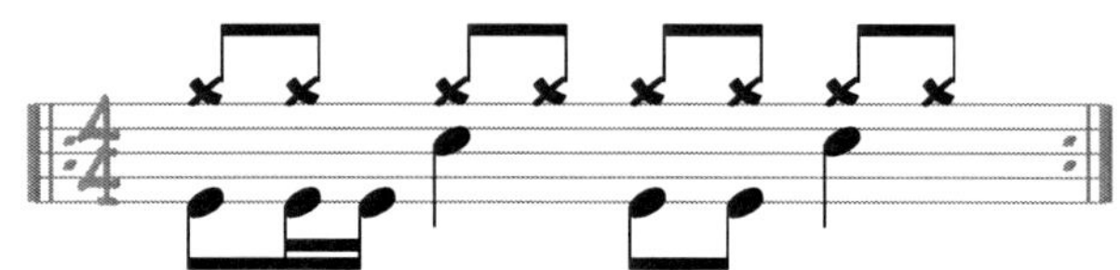

16

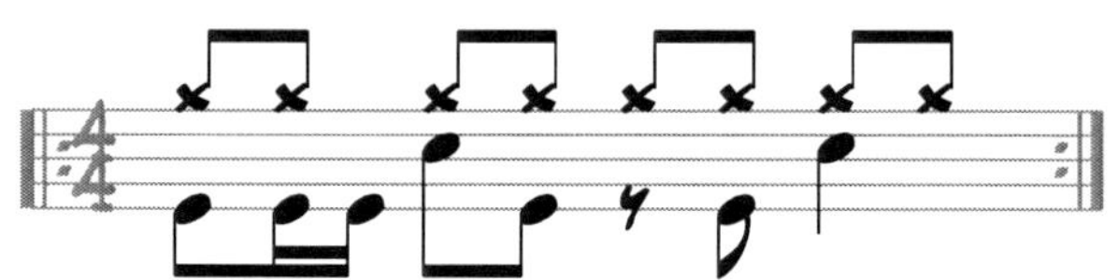

17

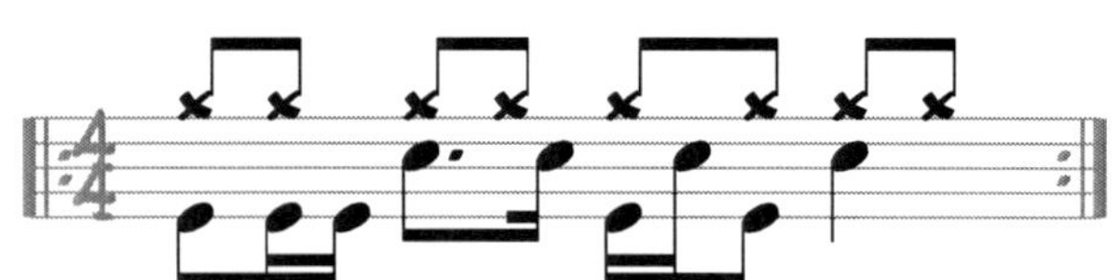

18

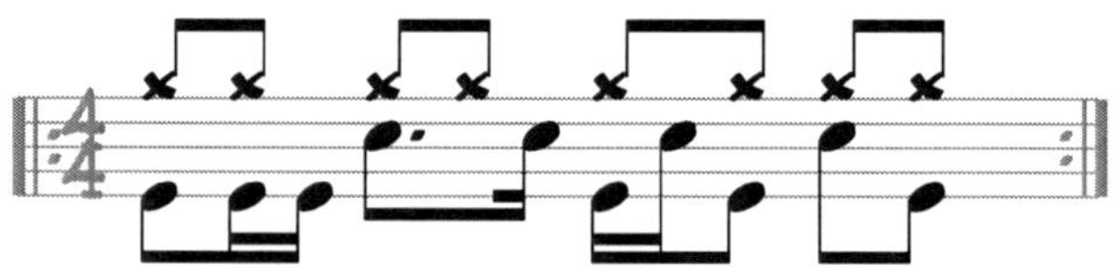

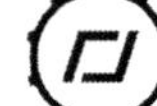

19

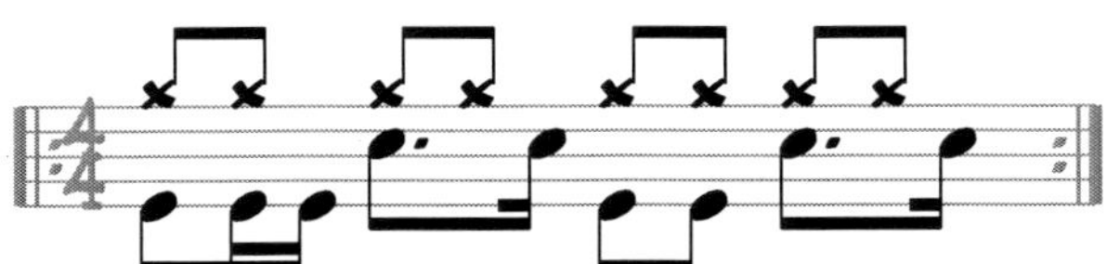

20

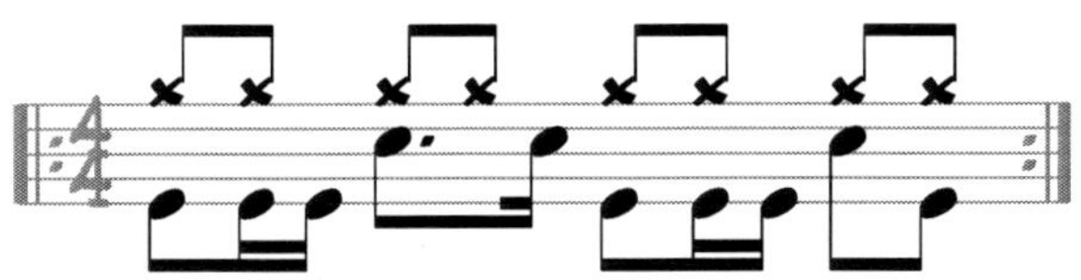

21

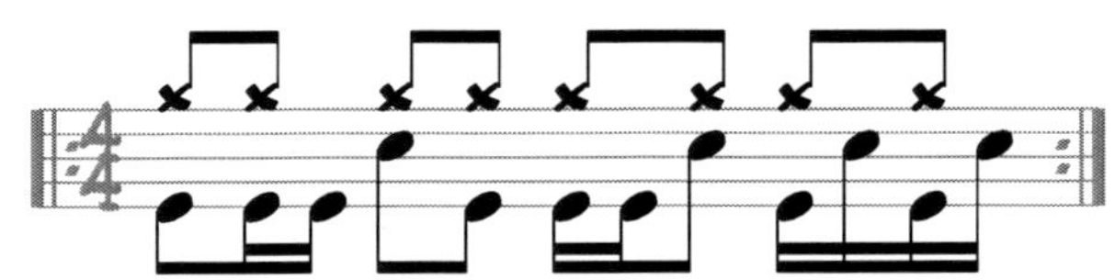

22

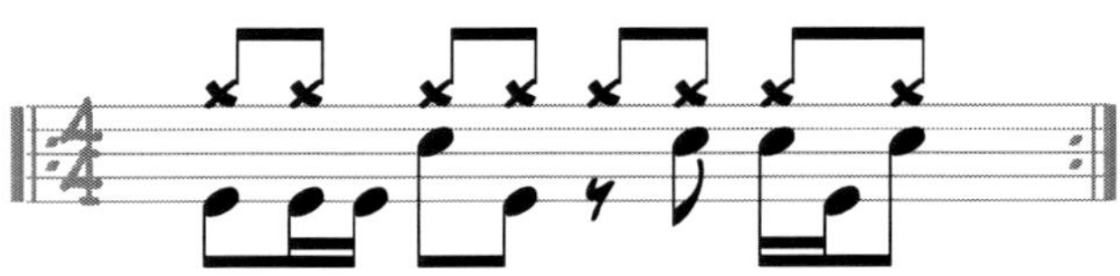

23

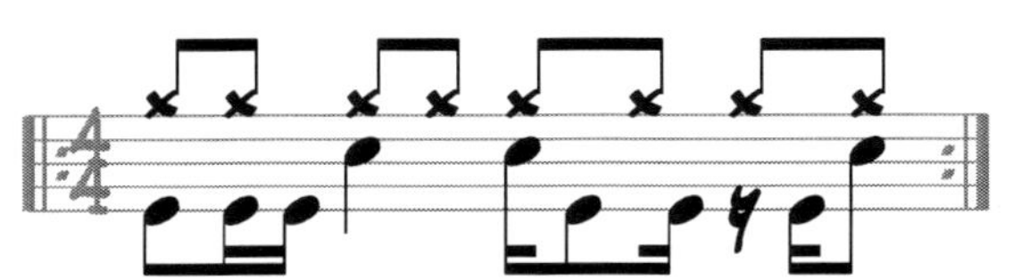

24

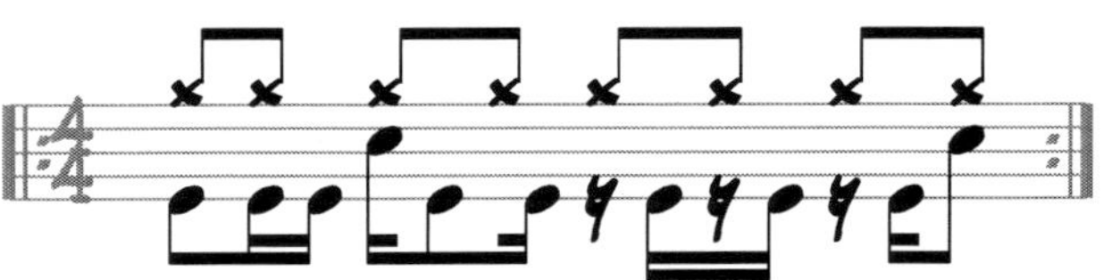

25

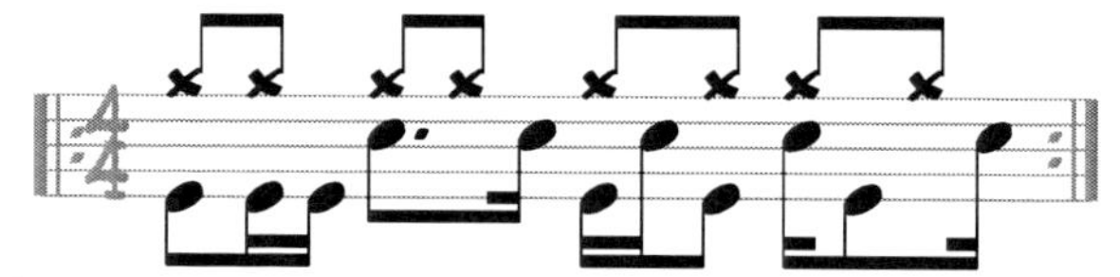

26

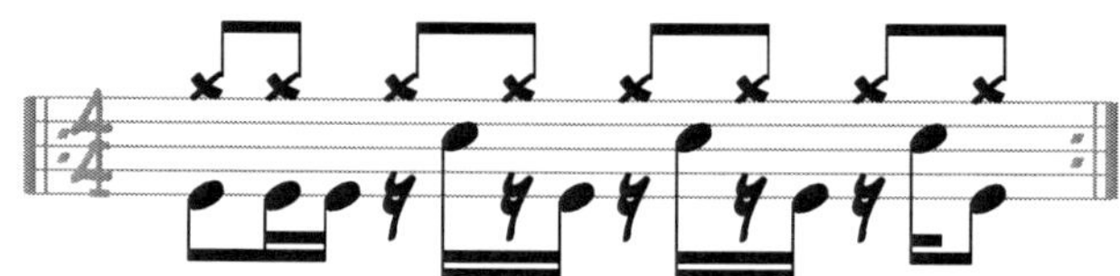

27

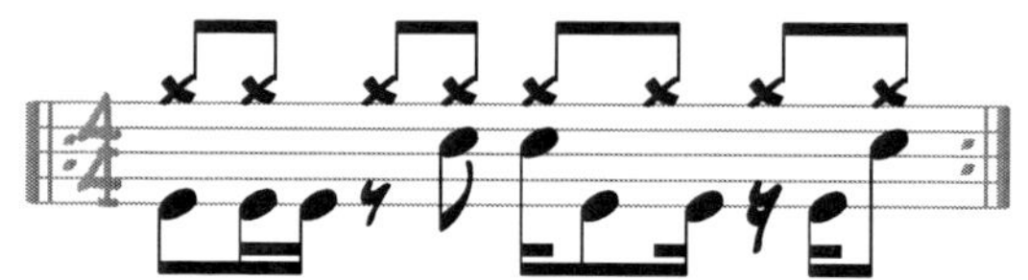

28

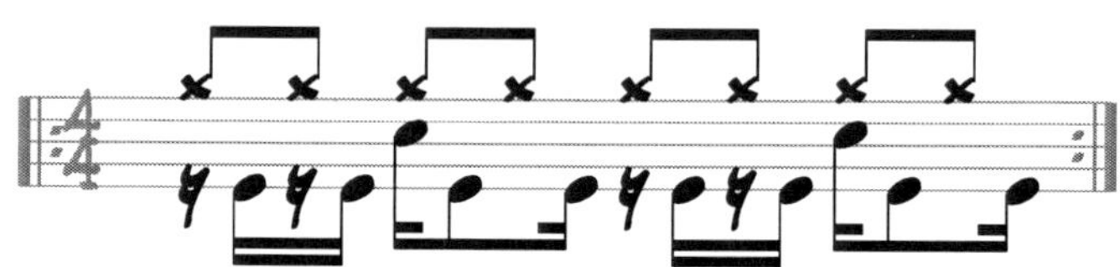

29

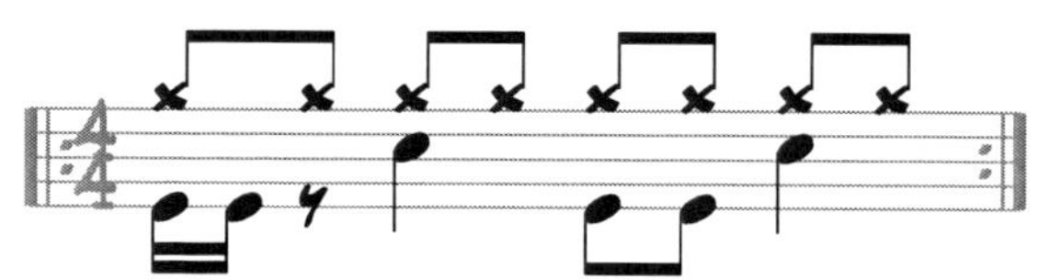

30

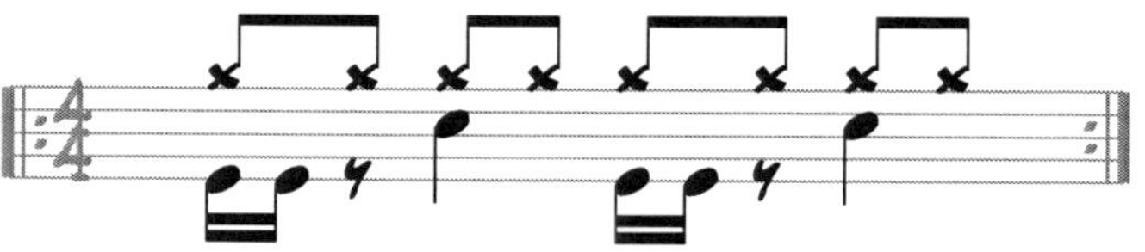

(31)

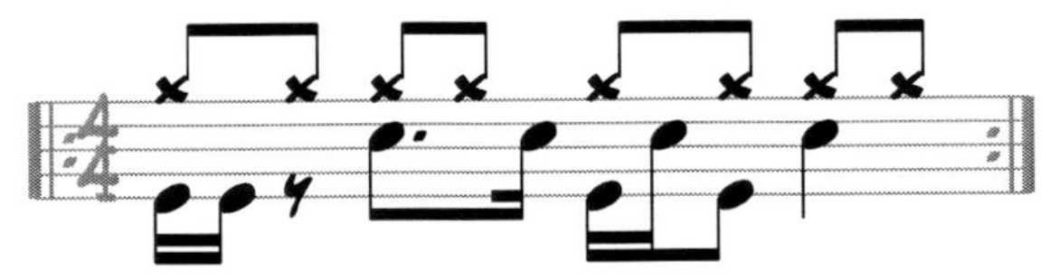

(32)

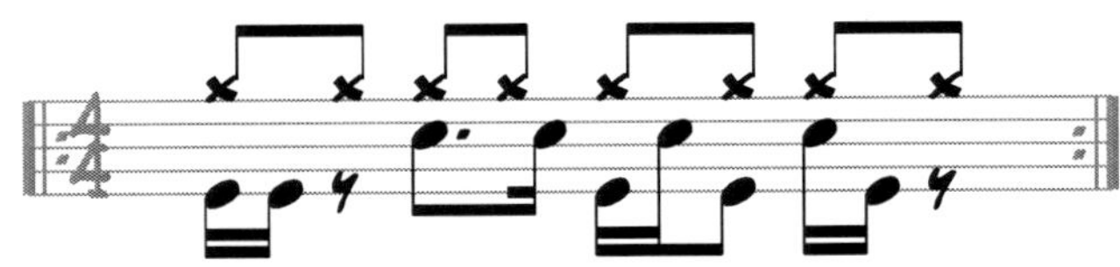

(33)

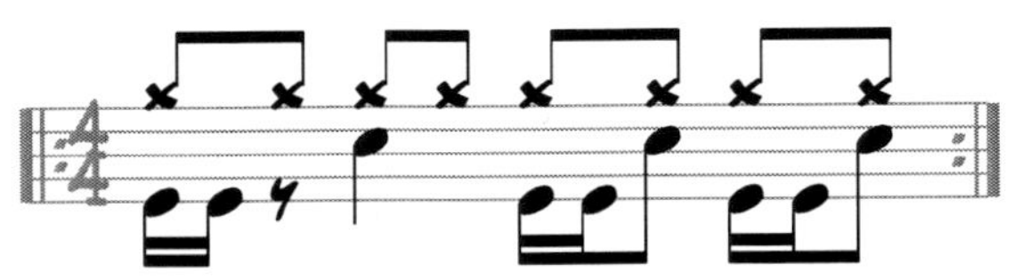

(34)

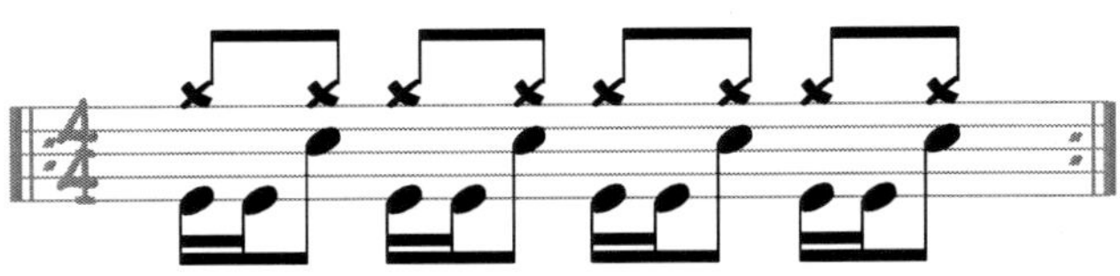

(35)

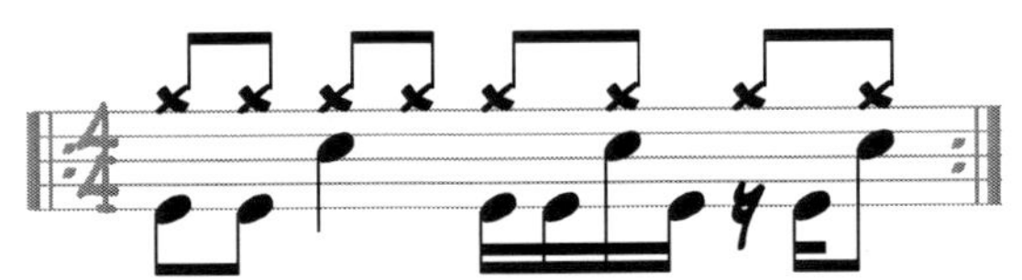

(36)

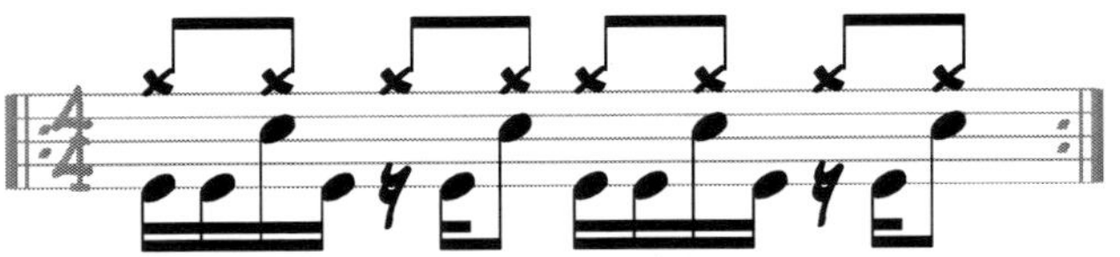

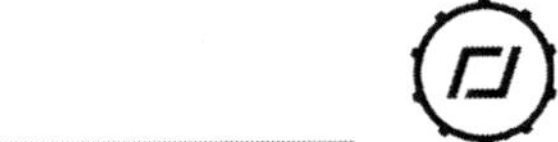

37

38

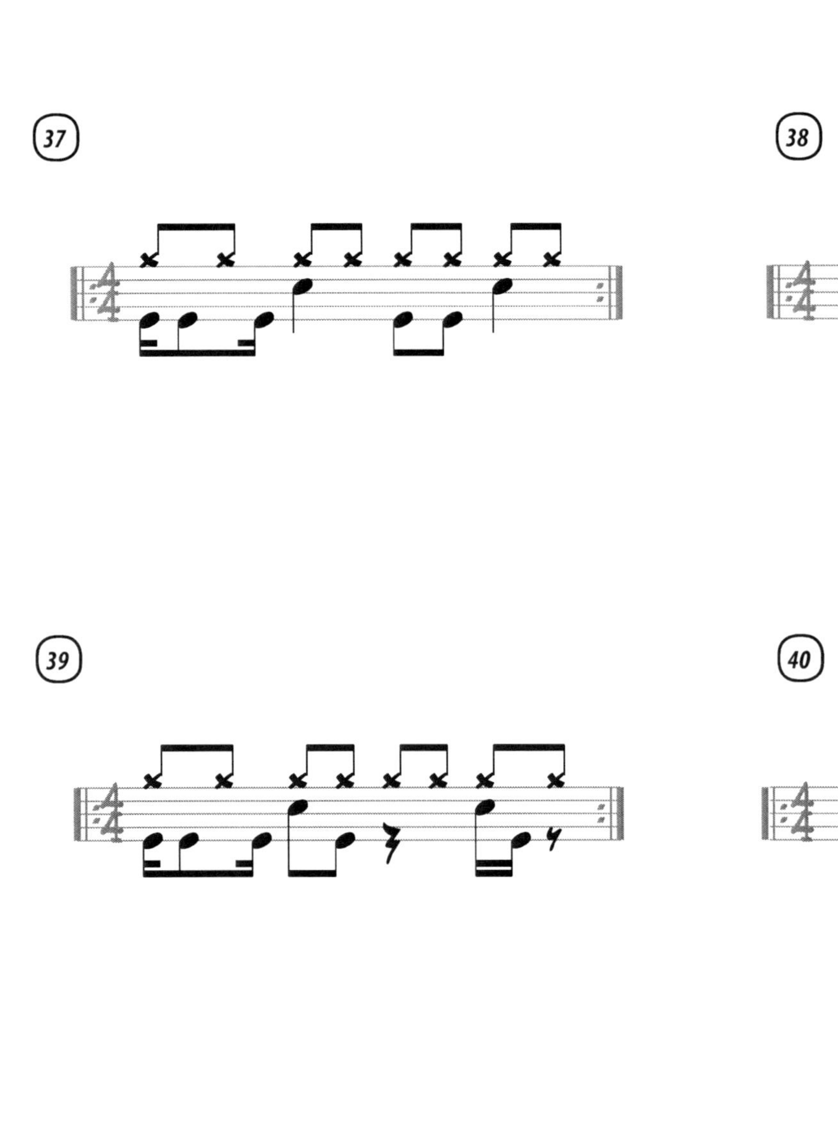

39

40

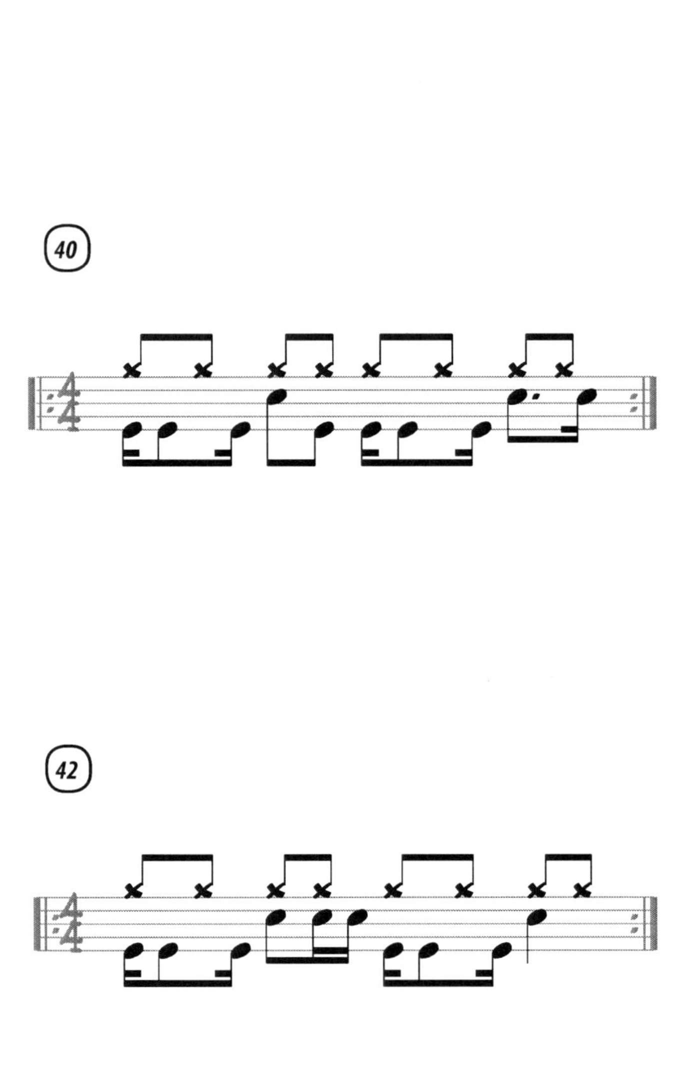

41

42

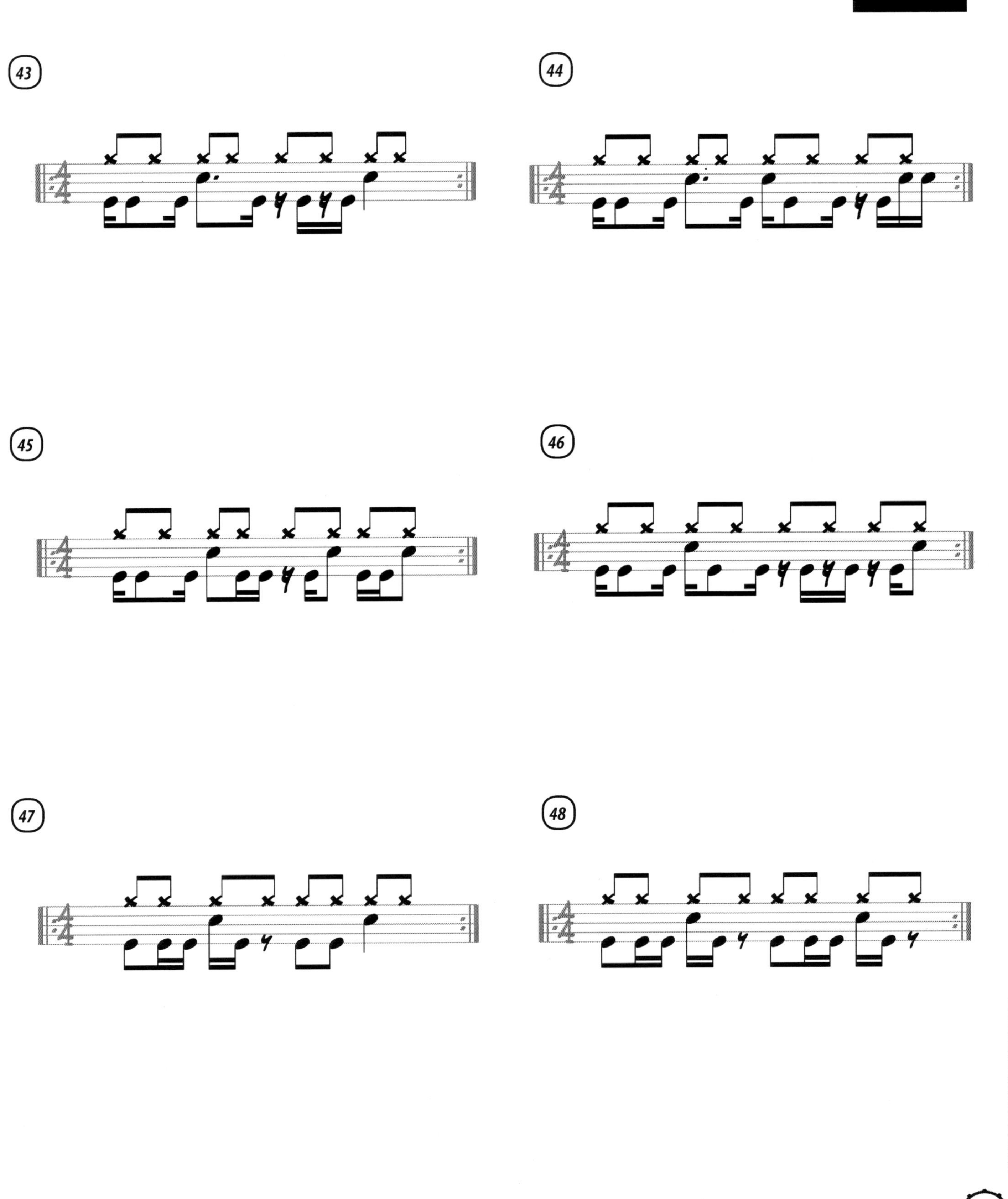
43
44
45
46
47
48

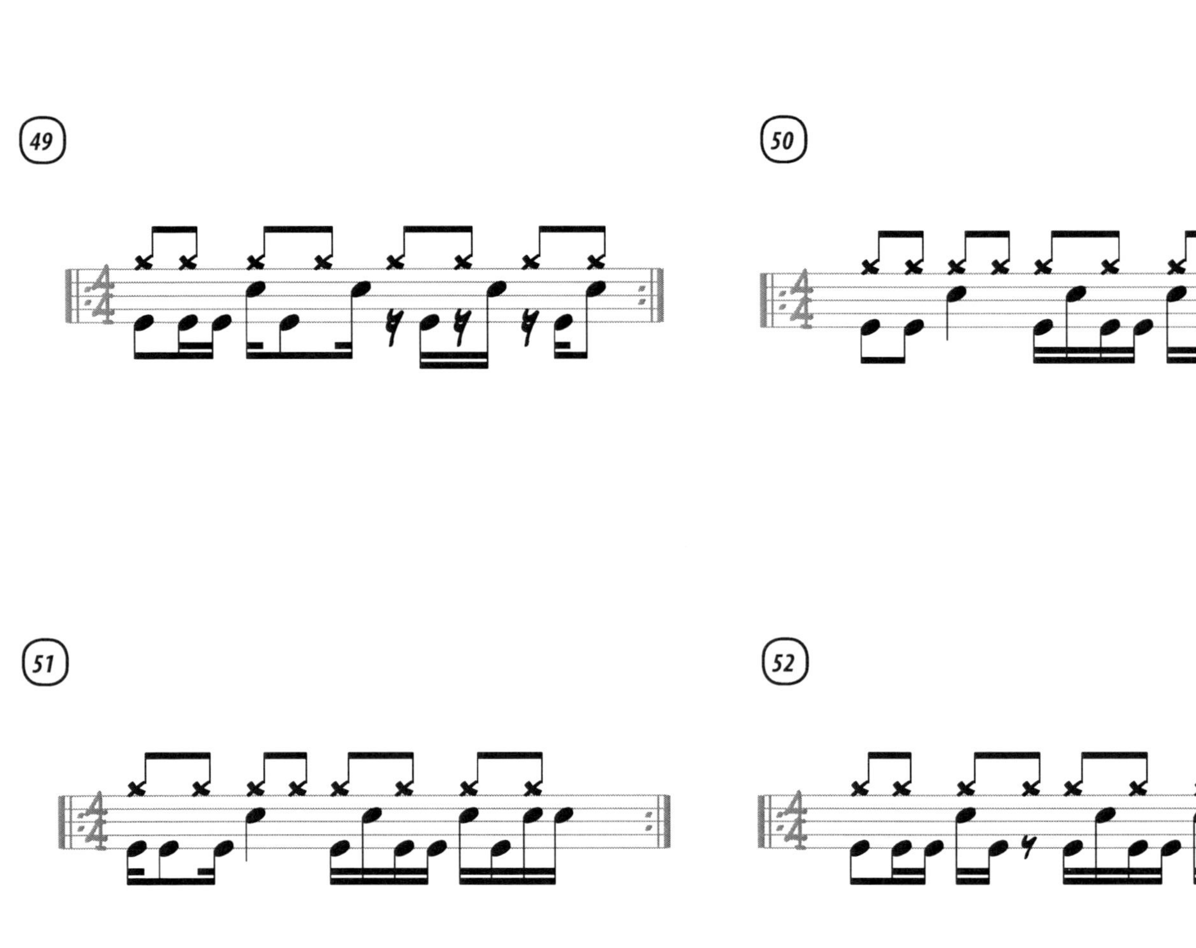
49
50
51
52

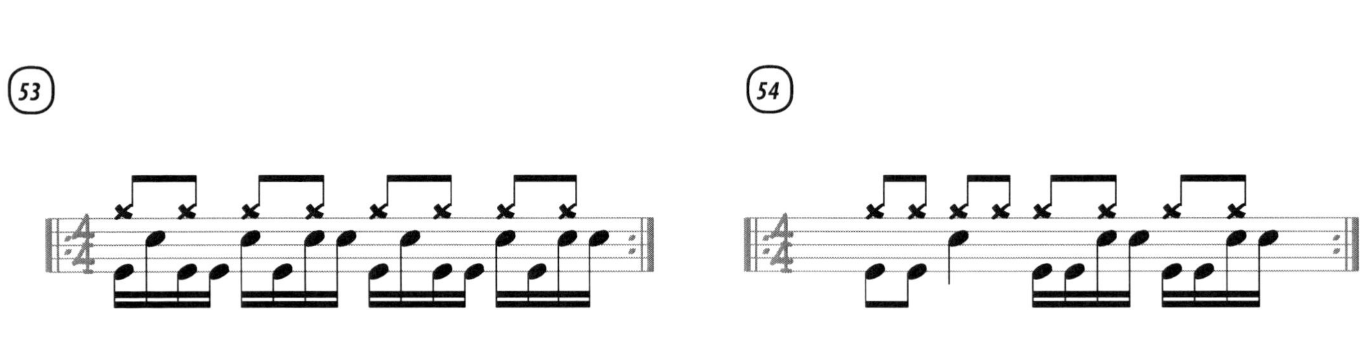
53
54

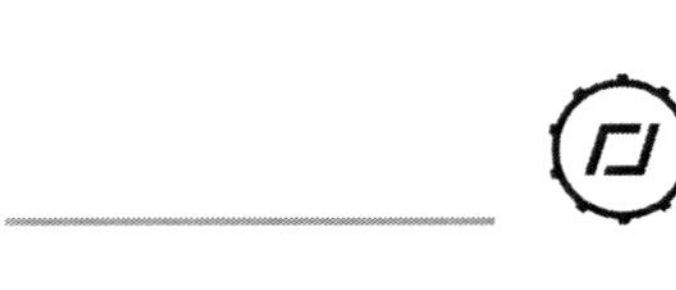

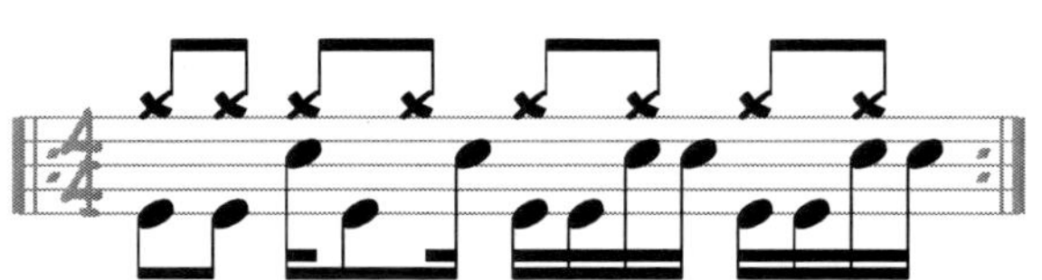

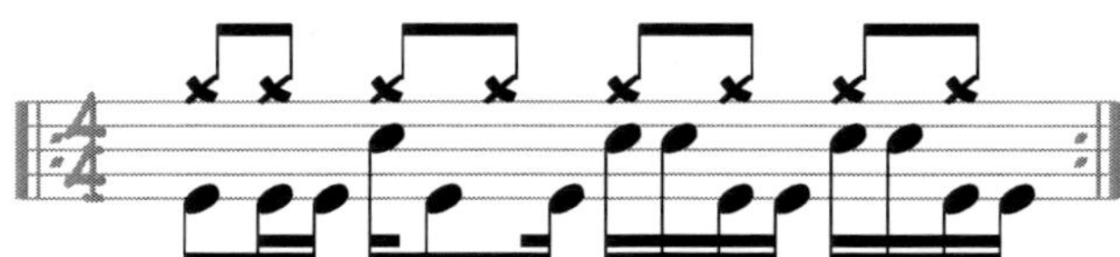

57

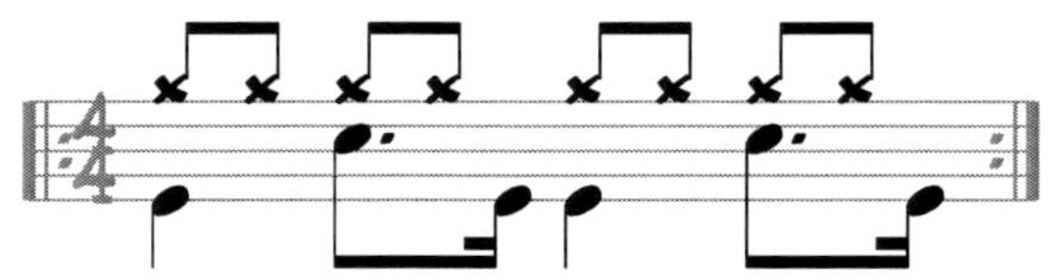

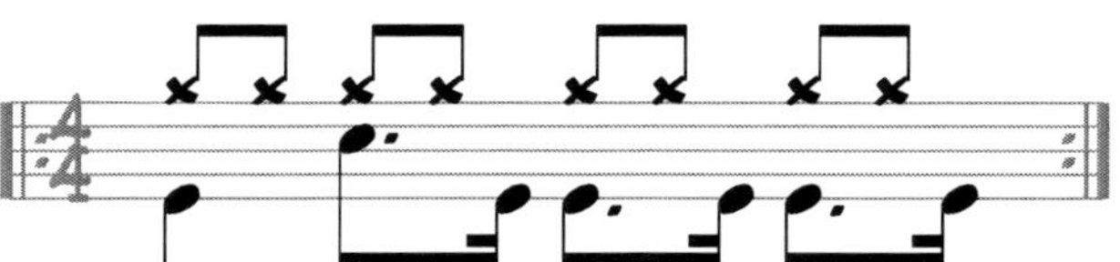

59

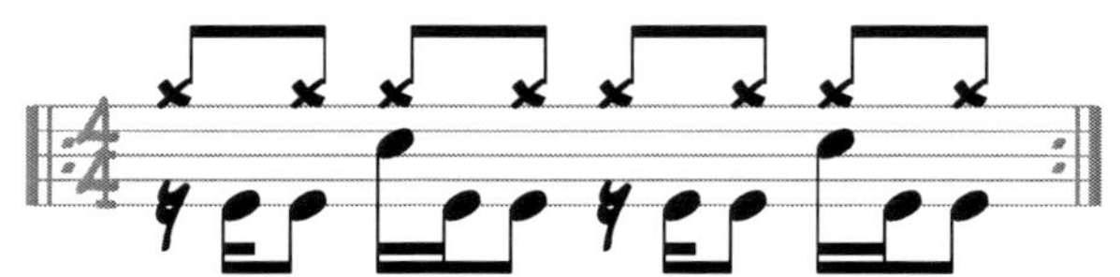

60

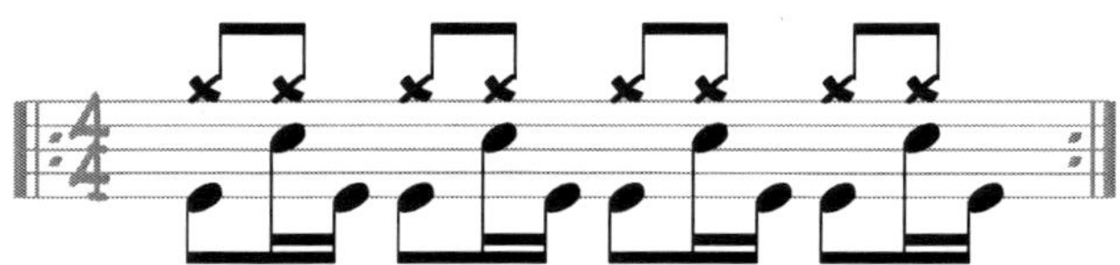

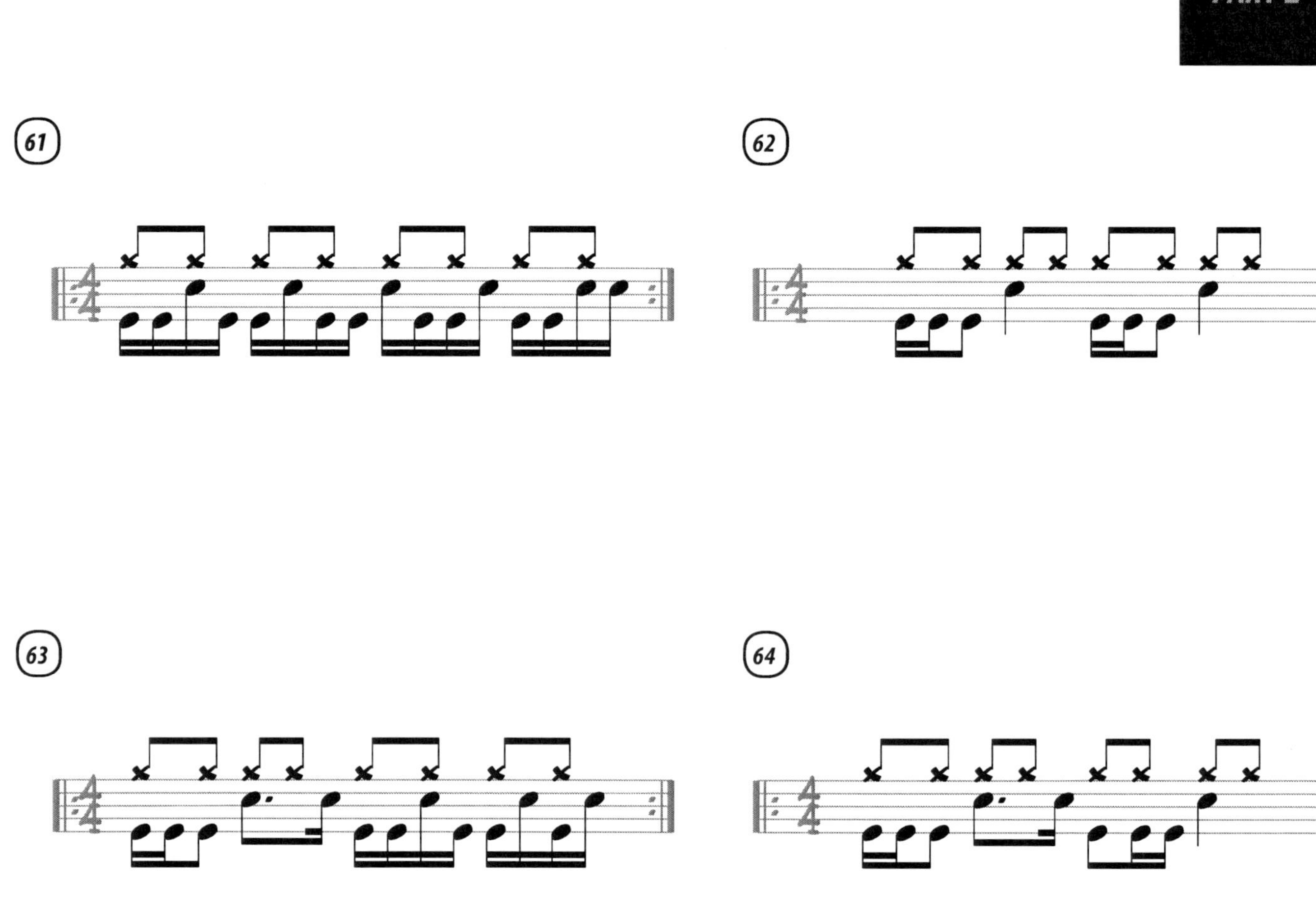

61
62
63
64

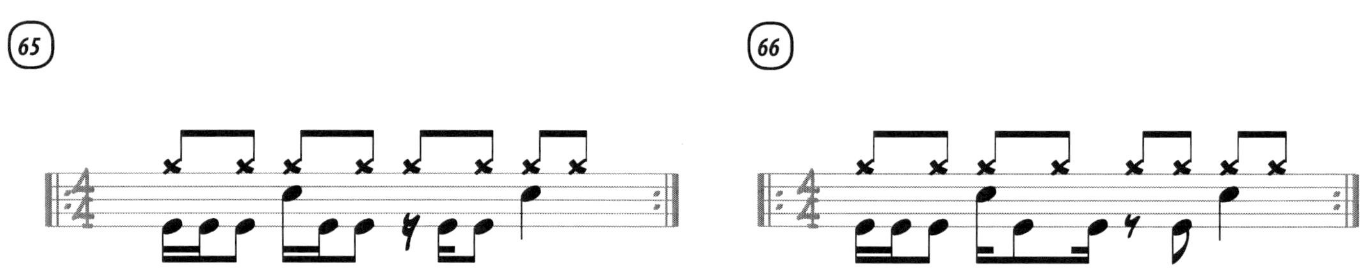

65
66

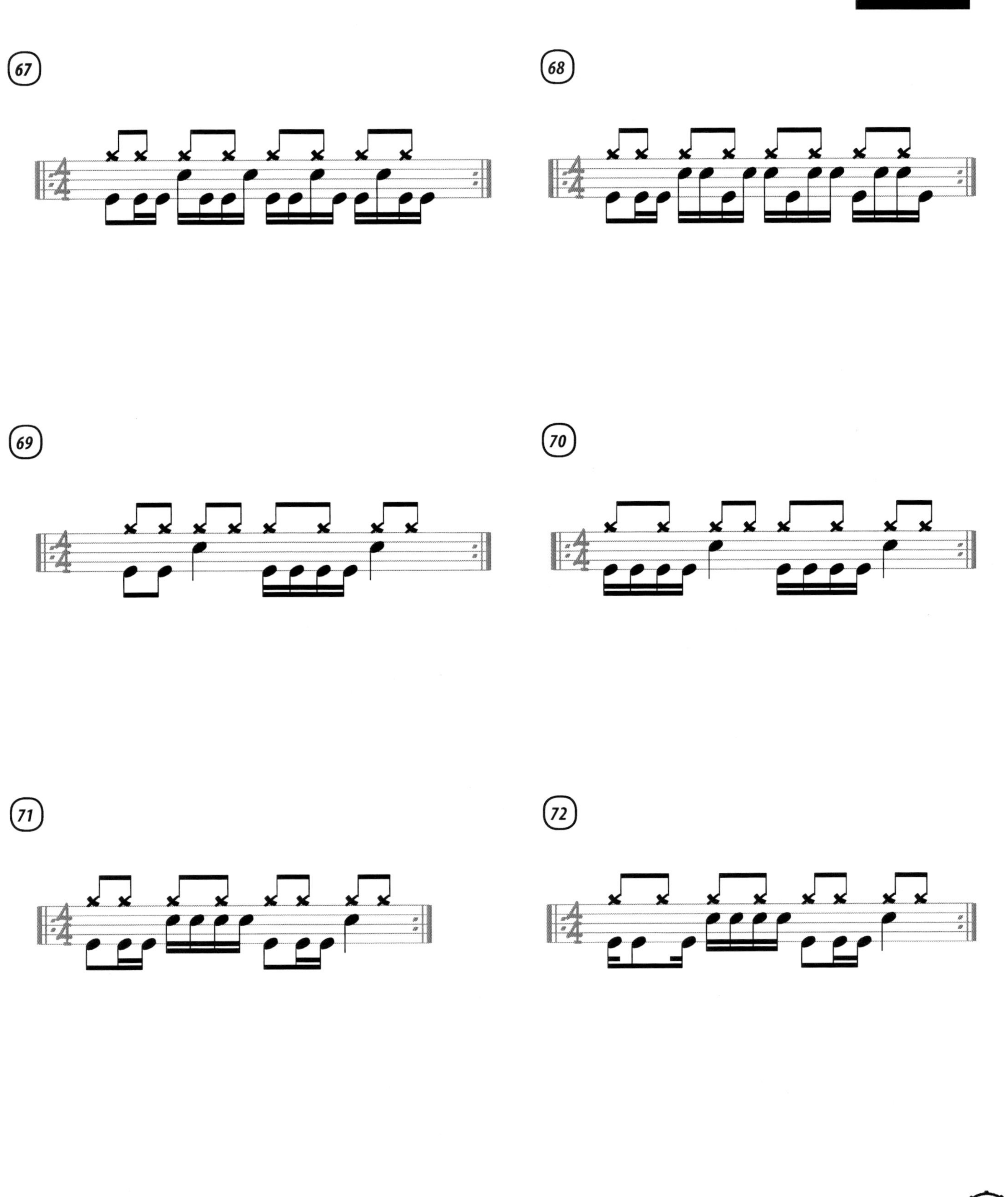
67
68
69
70
71
72

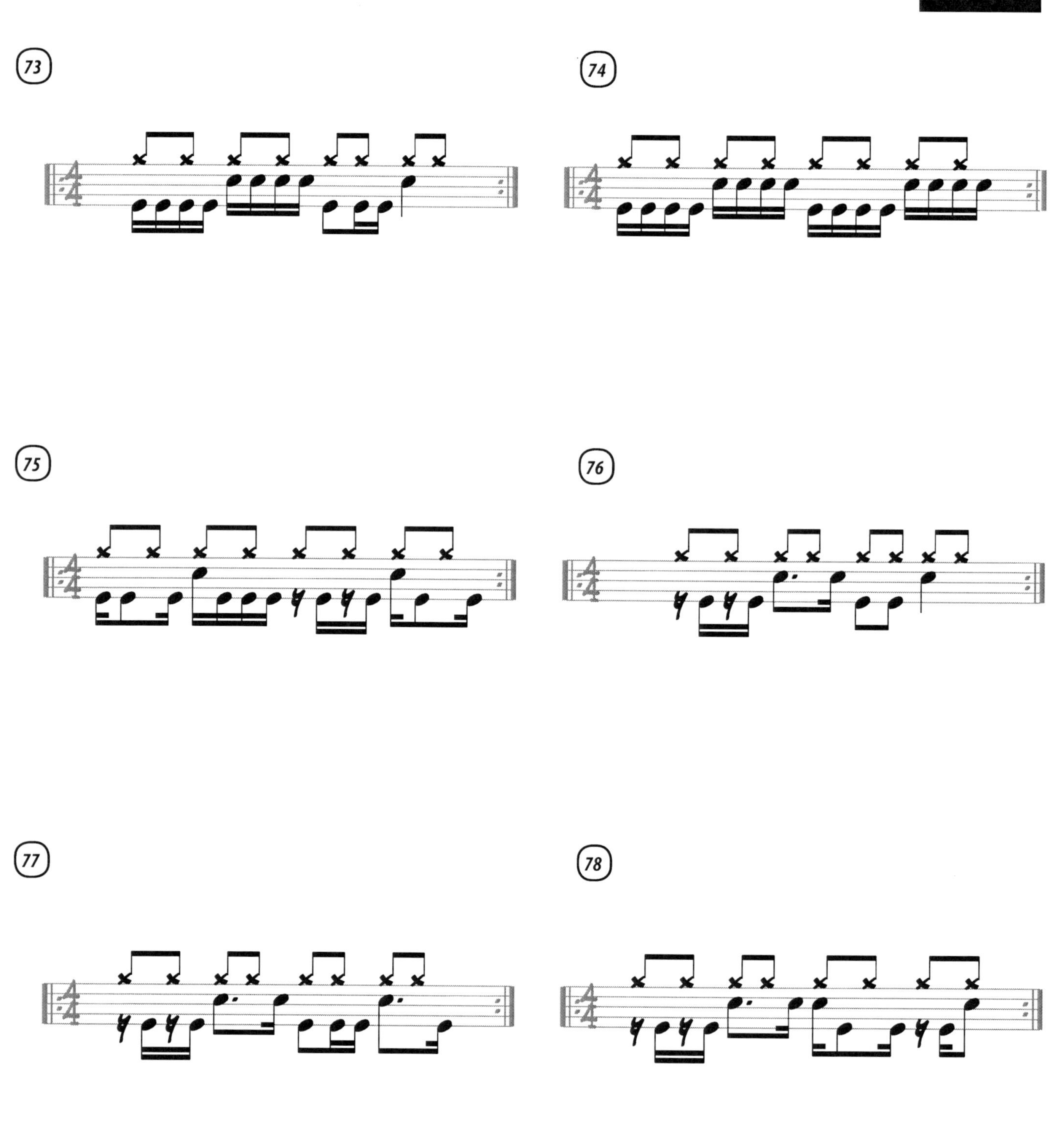
73
74
75
76
77
78

79

80

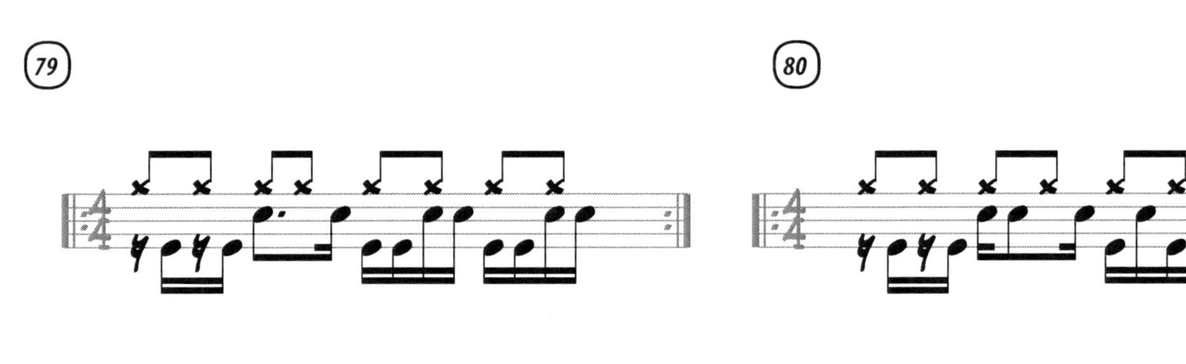

81

82

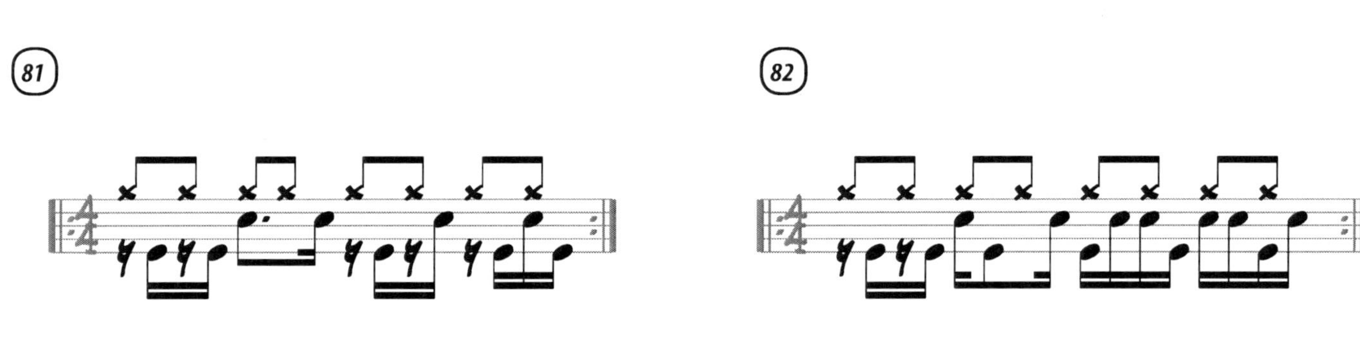

83

84

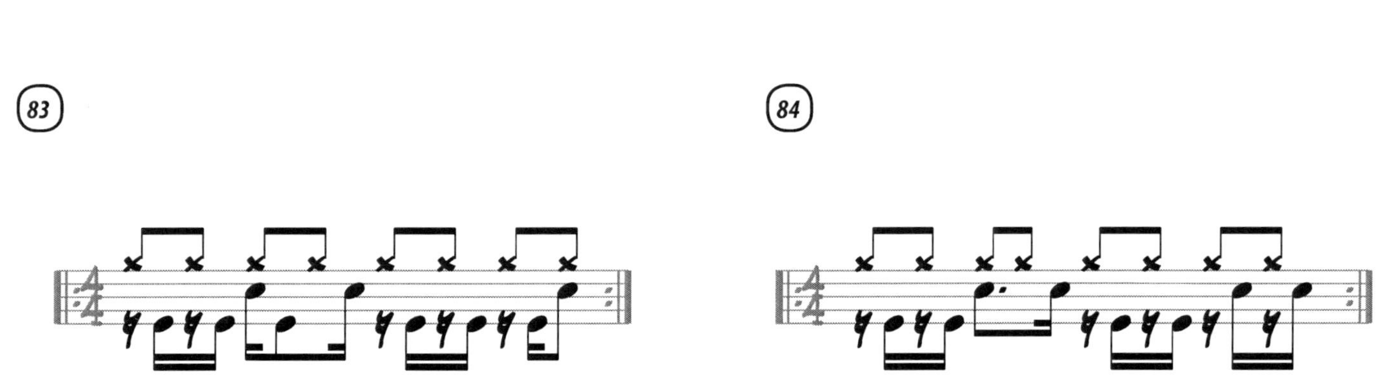

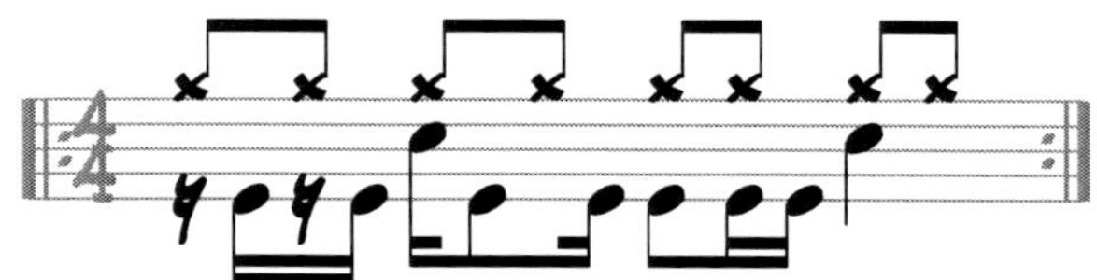

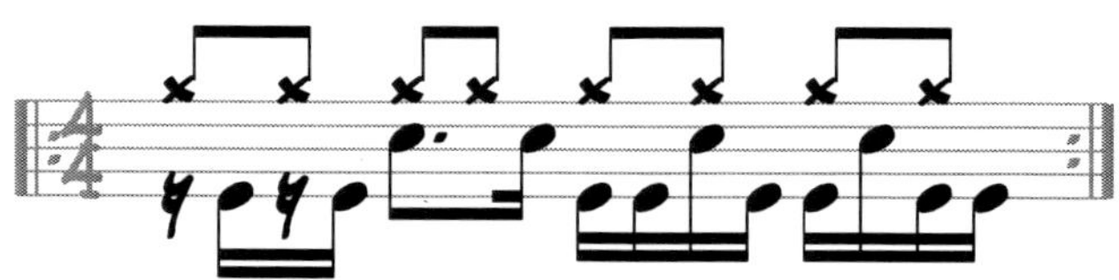

87

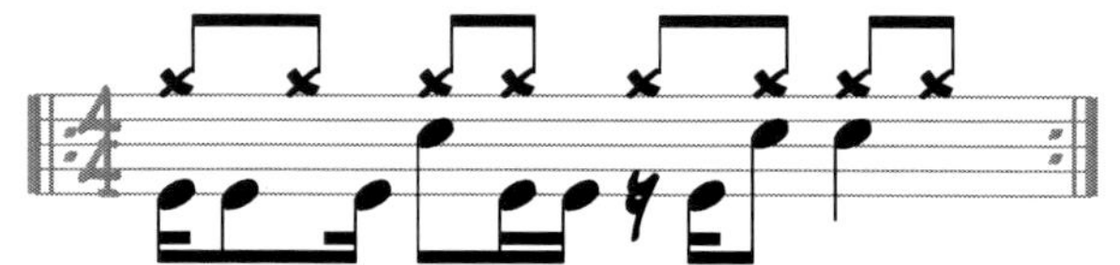

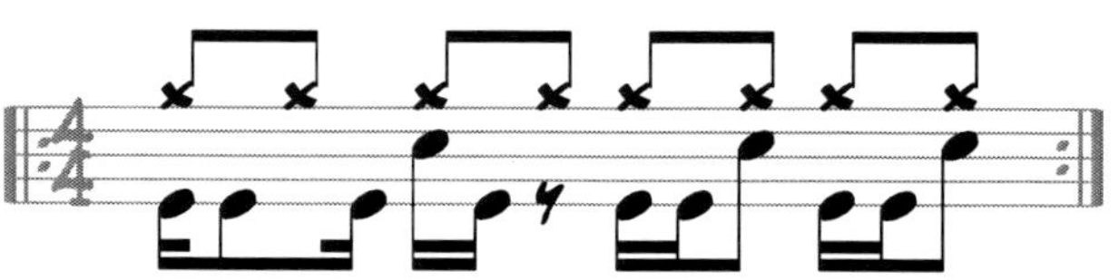

89

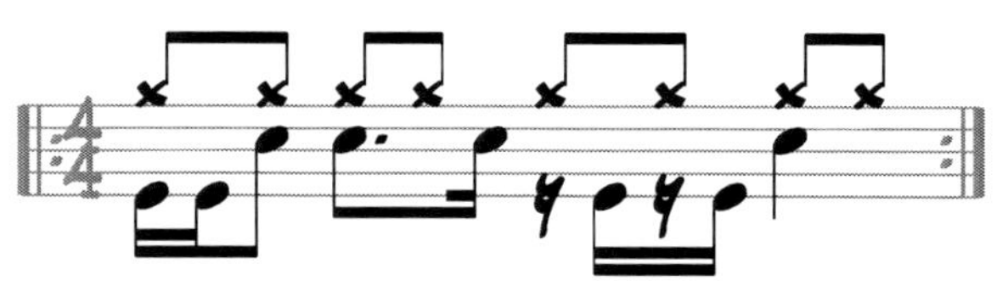

90

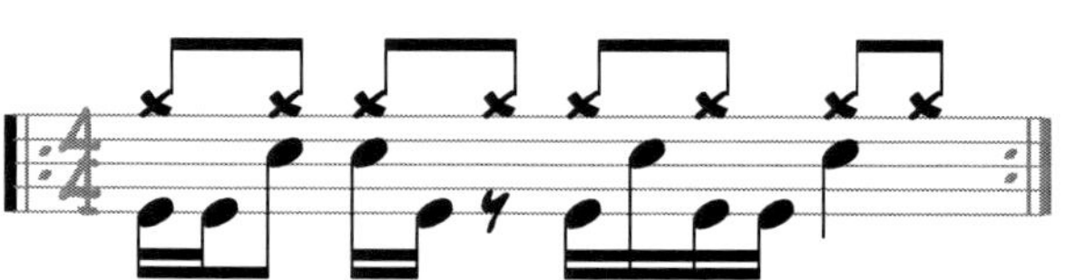

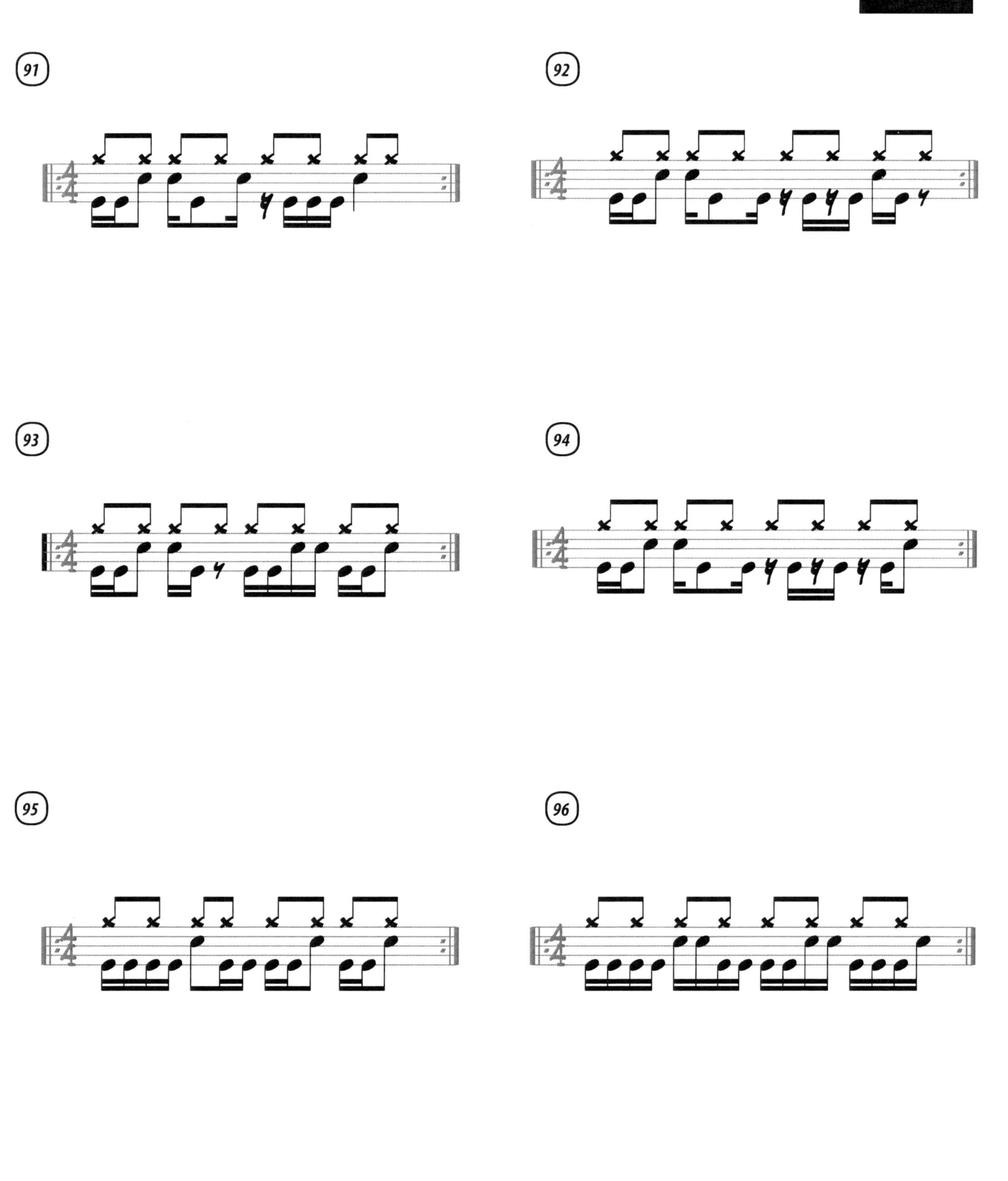
91
92
93
94
95
96

97

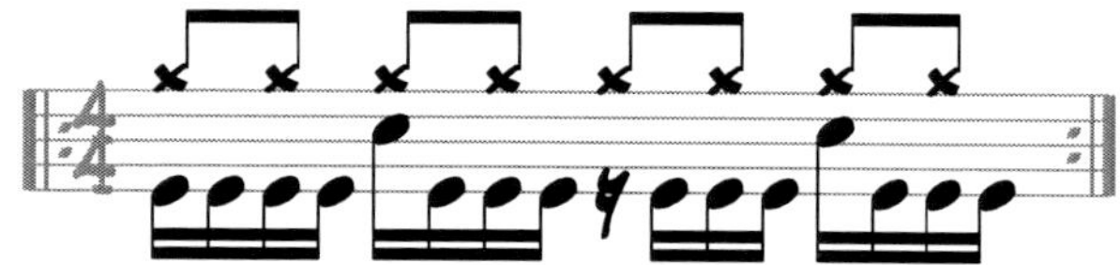

98

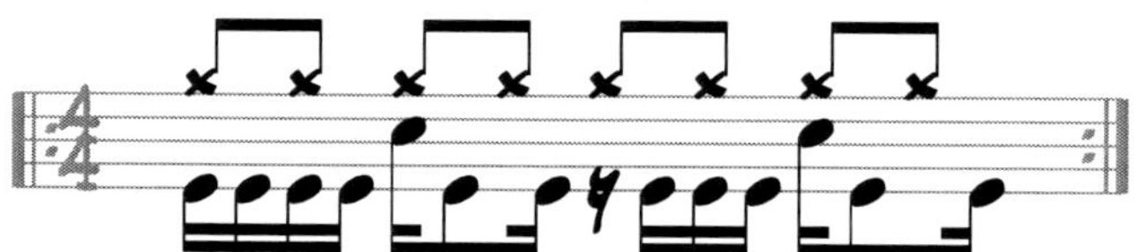

99

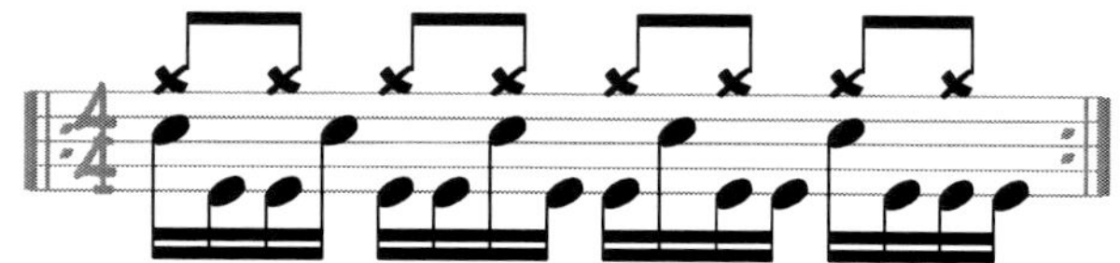

100

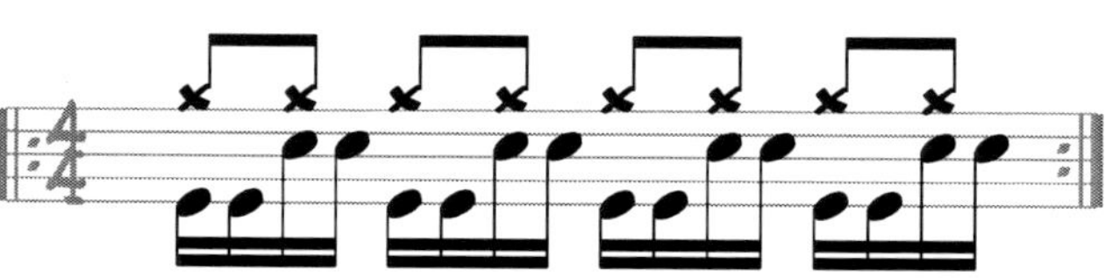

PART 3

COMBINATIONS

3.1 OPEN HI-HAT COMBINATIONS

PART 3.1

1

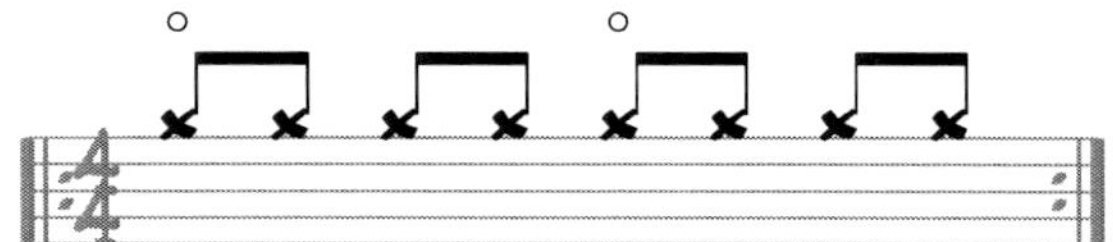

2

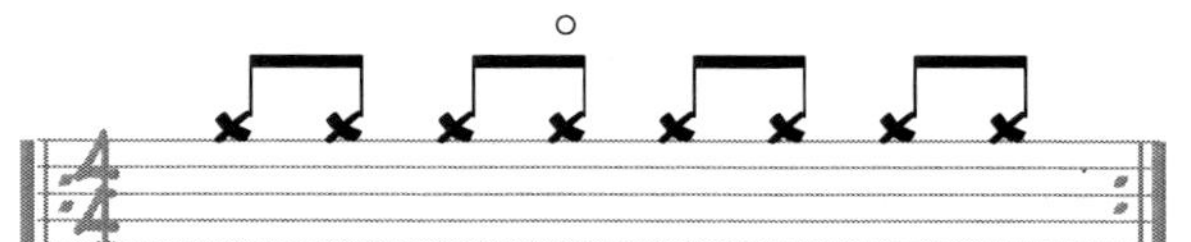

3

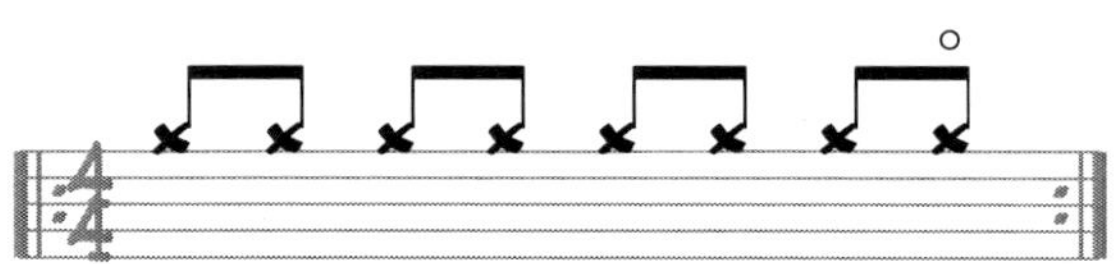

4

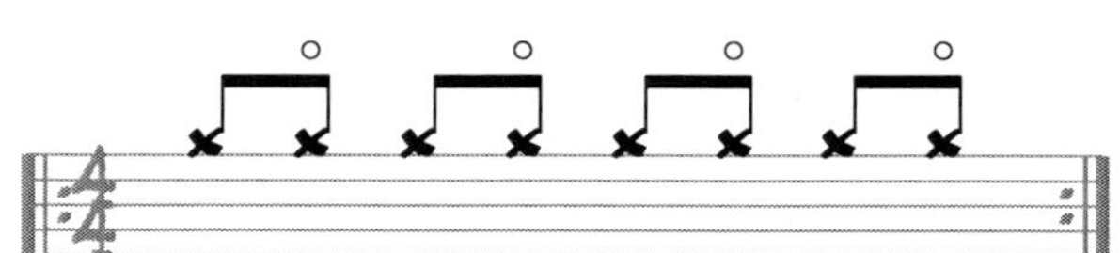

5

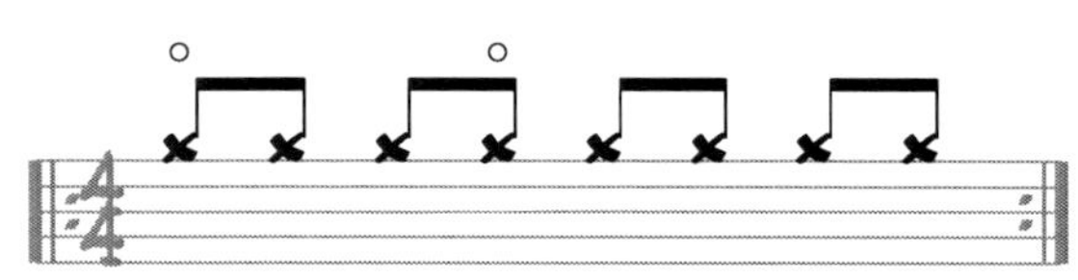

6

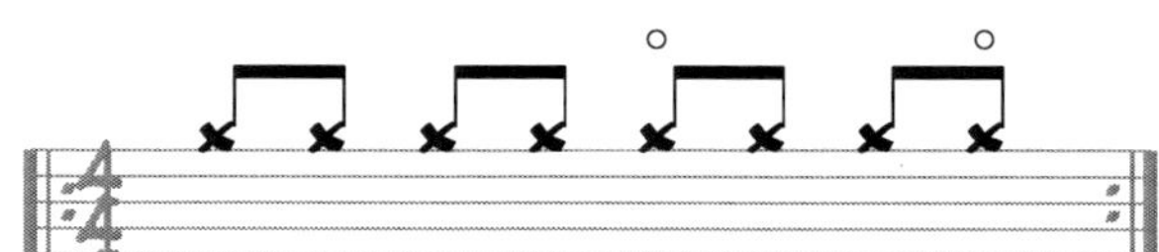

7

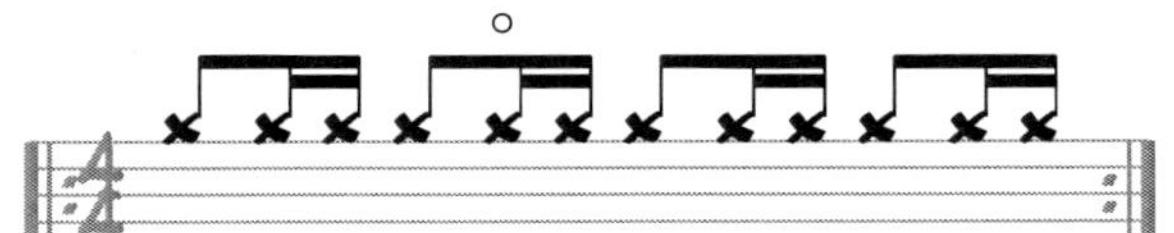

8

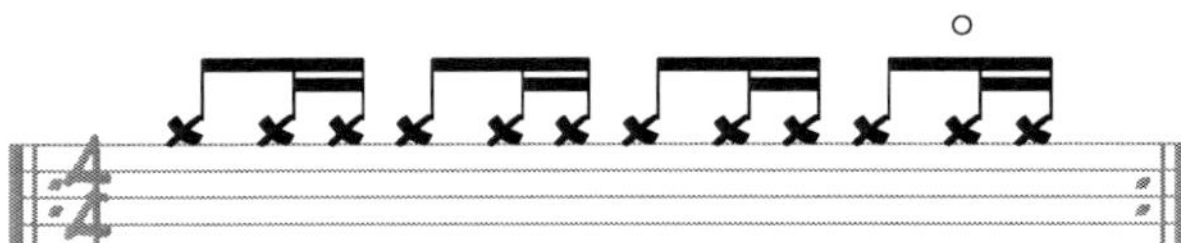

9

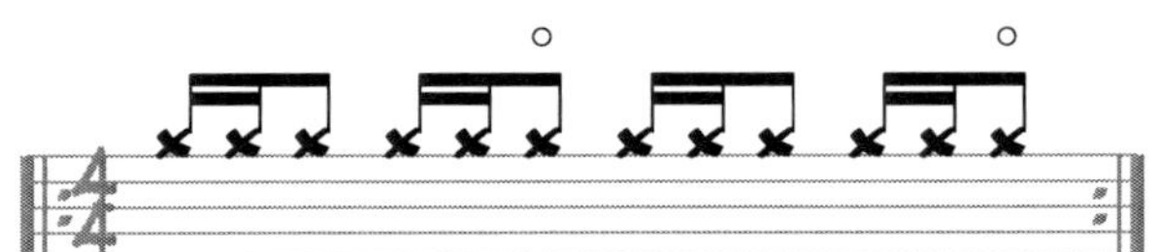

10

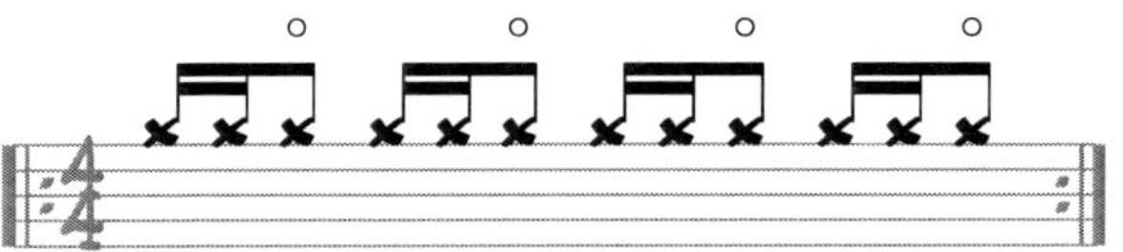

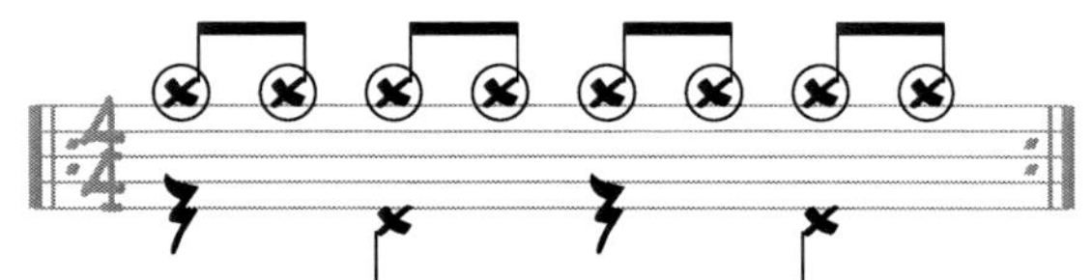

2

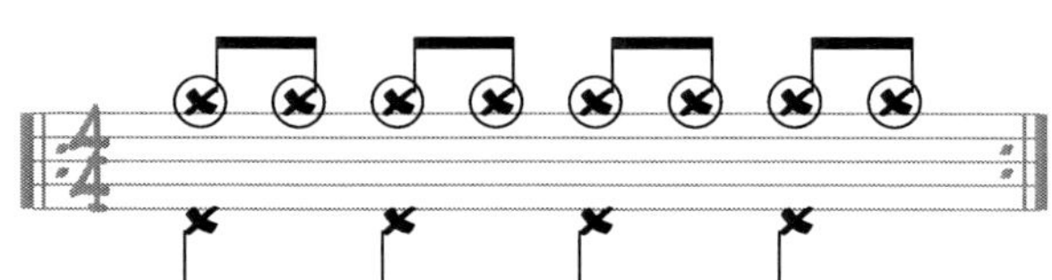

3

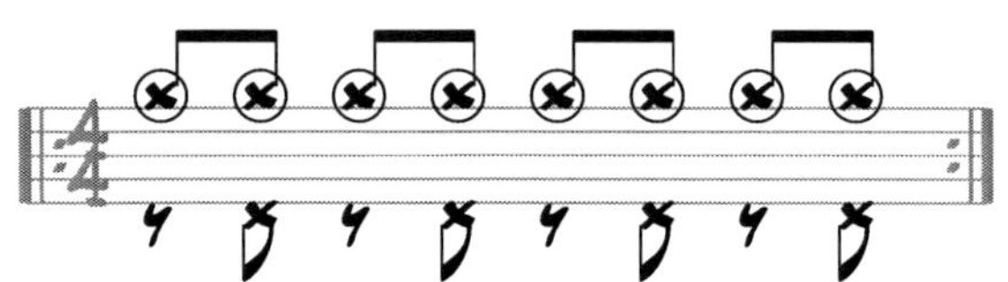

4

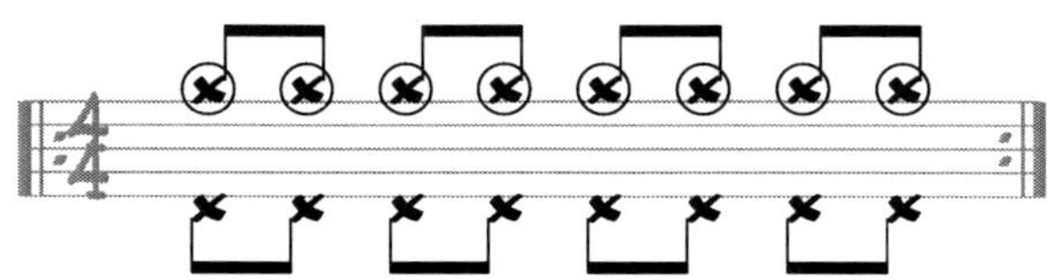

5

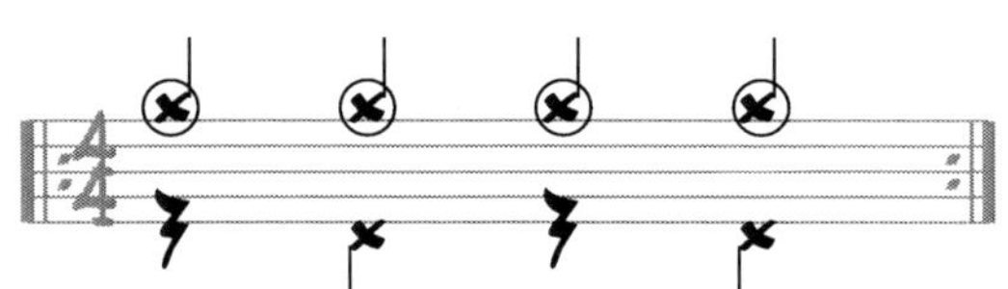

6

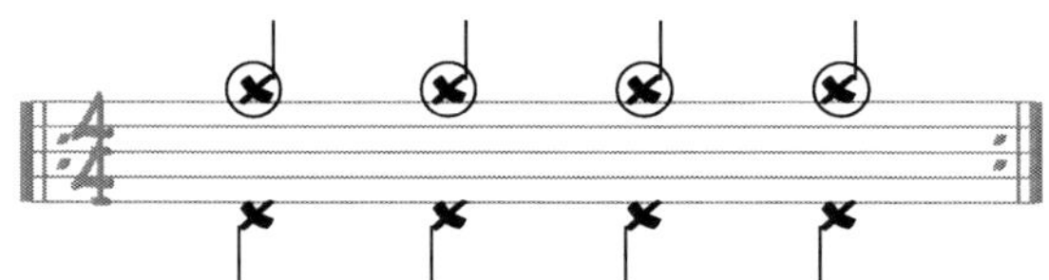

7

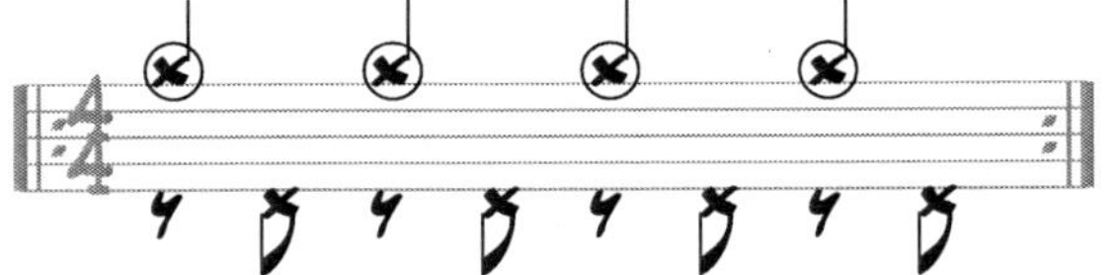

8

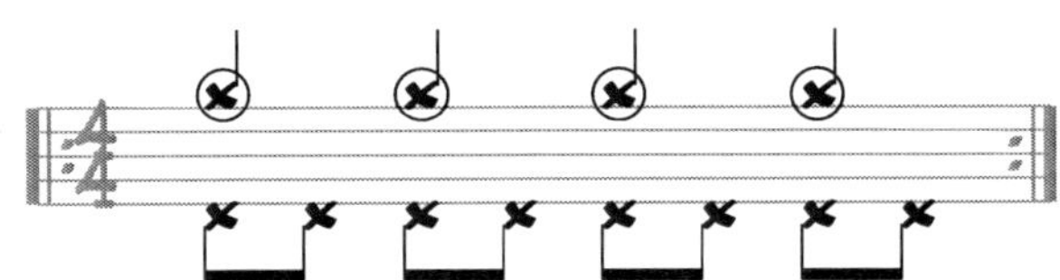

9

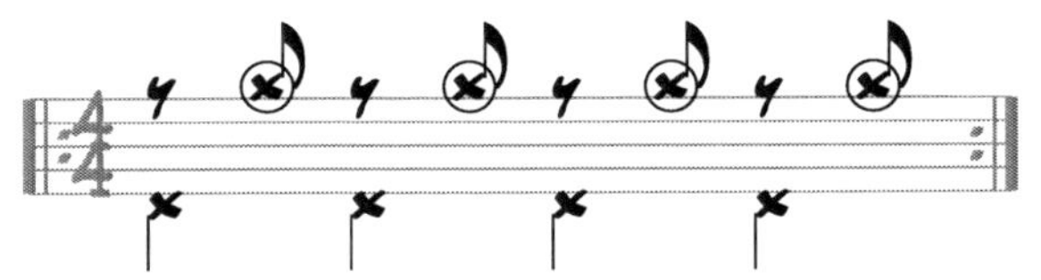

10

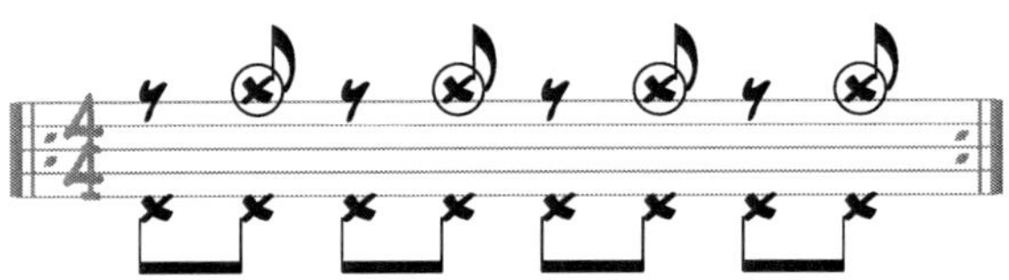

11

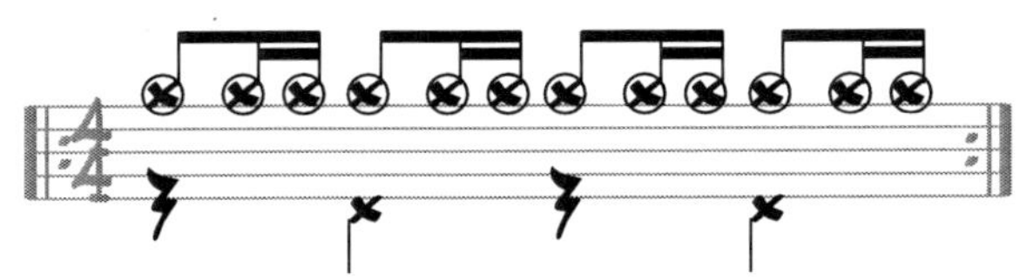

12

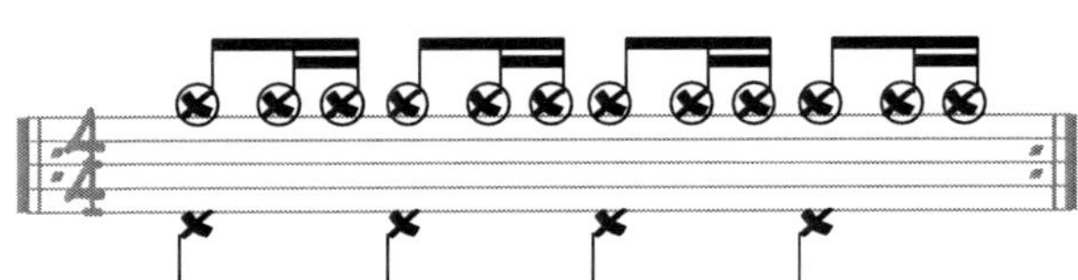

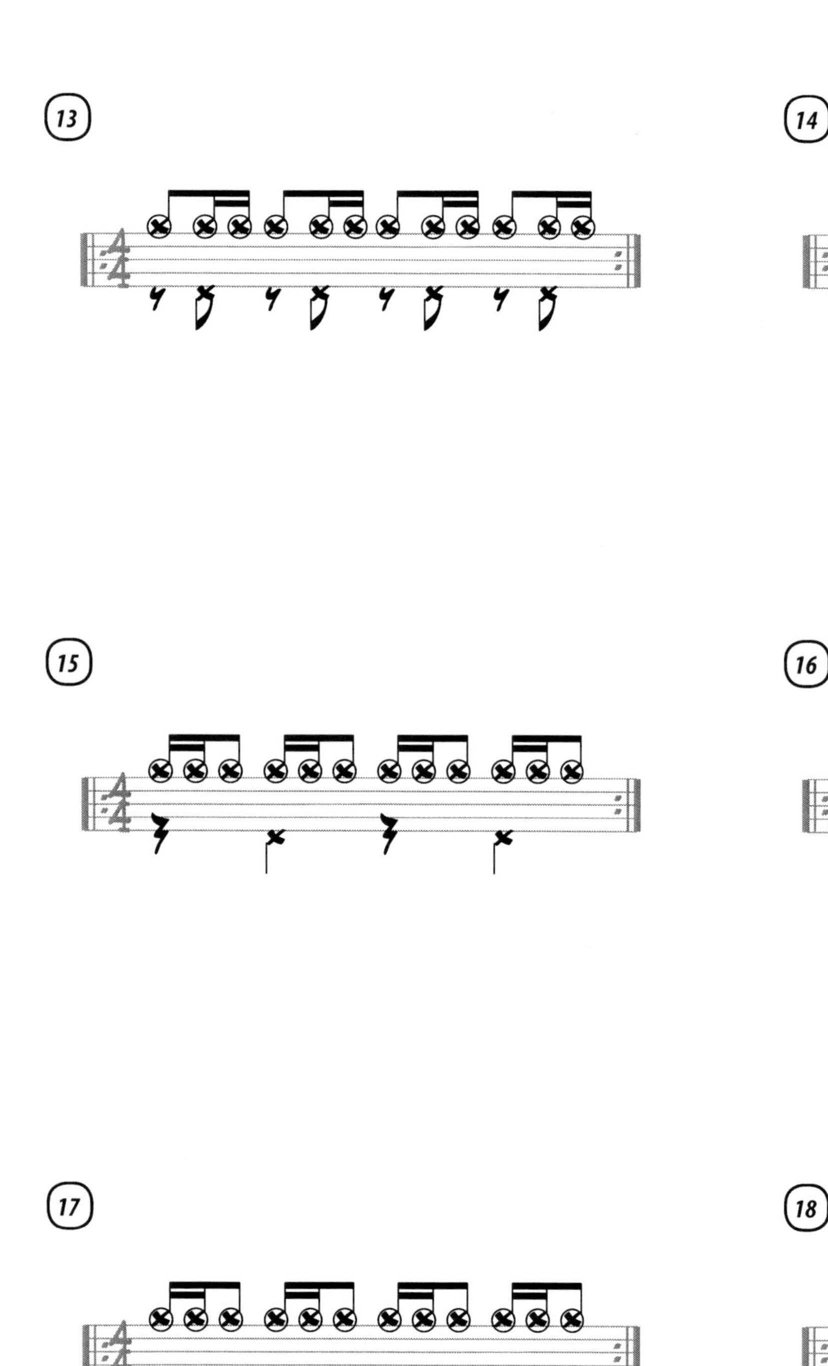
13
15
17

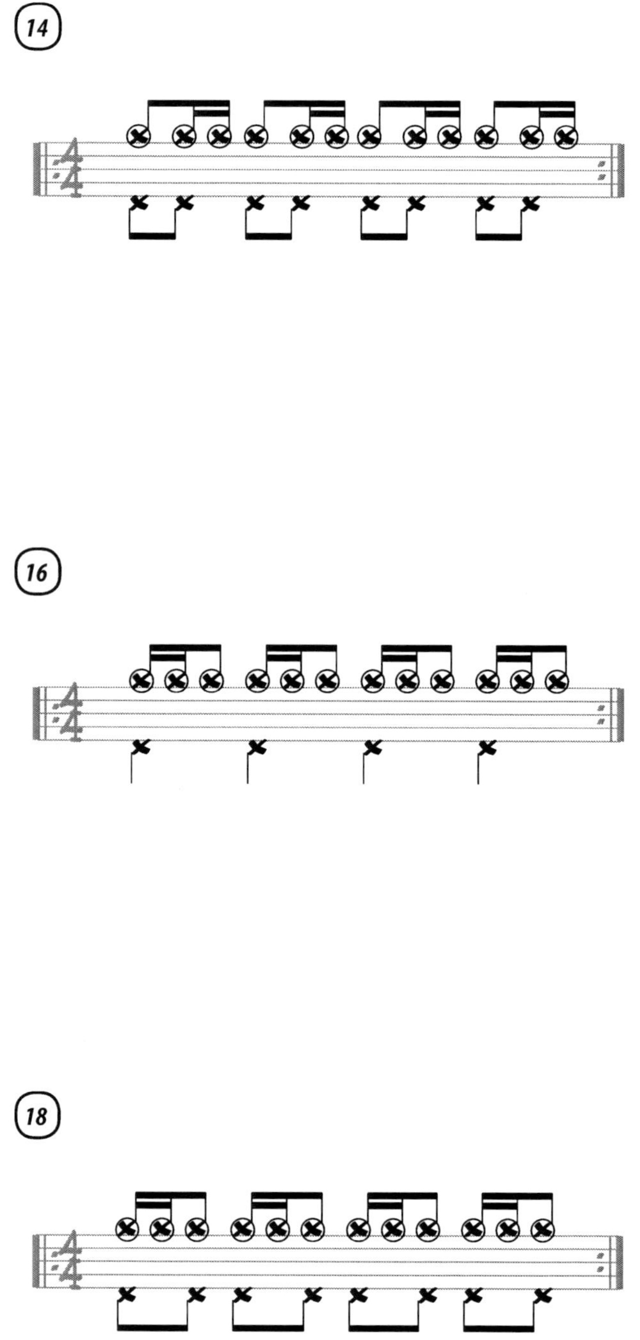
14
16
18

19

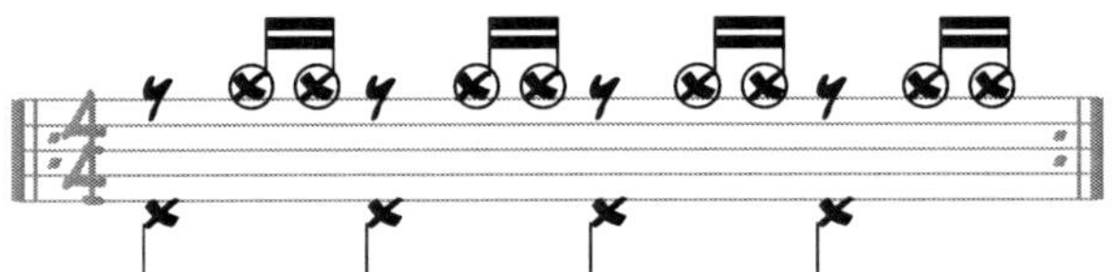

20

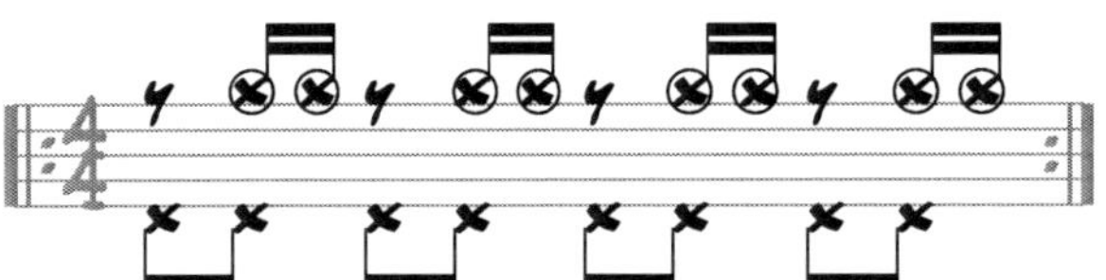

3.3 SIXTEENTH-NOTE COMBINATIONS

1

Count: 1 e + a 2 e + a 3 e + a 4 e + a

2

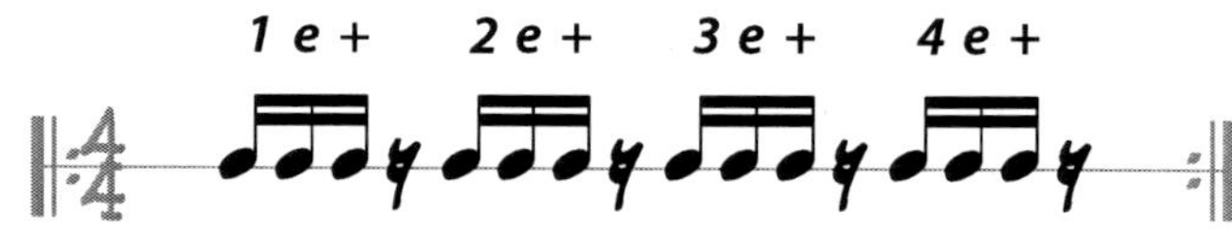

3

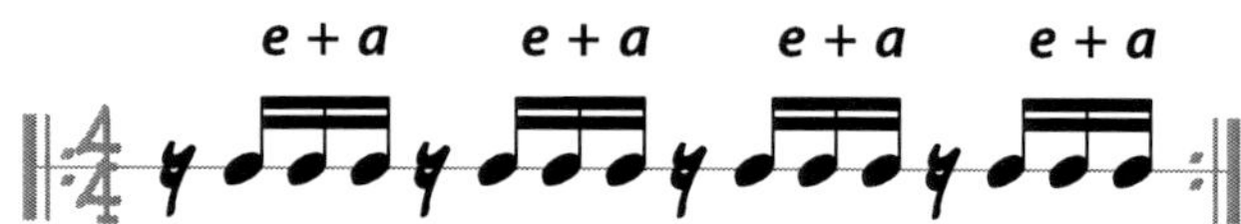

4

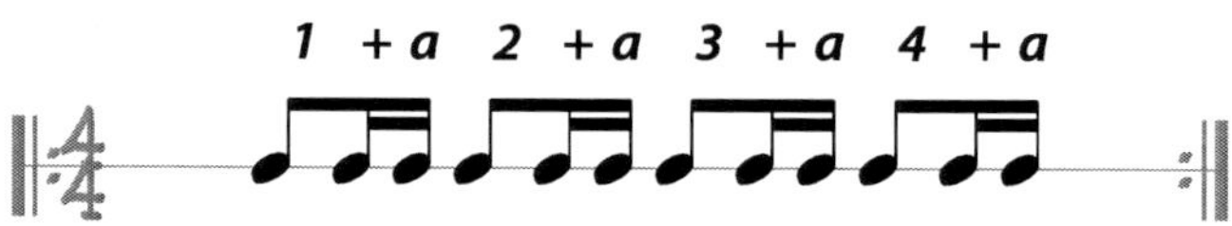

5

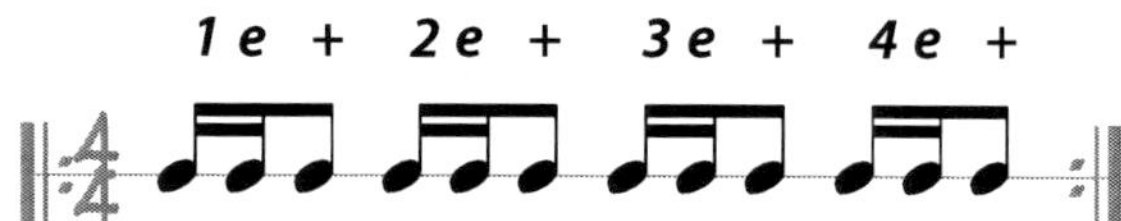

6

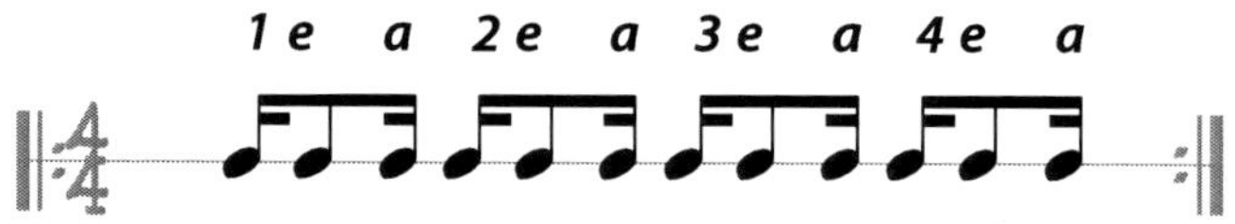

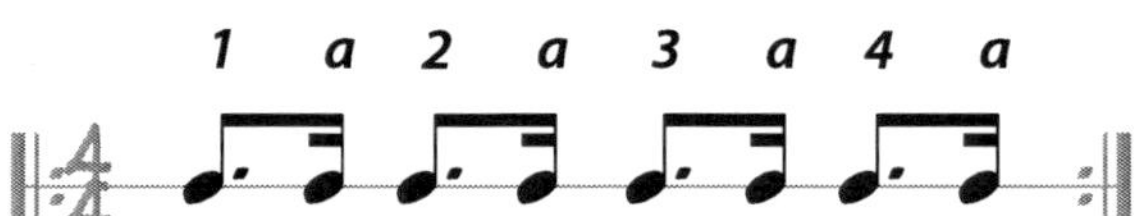

8

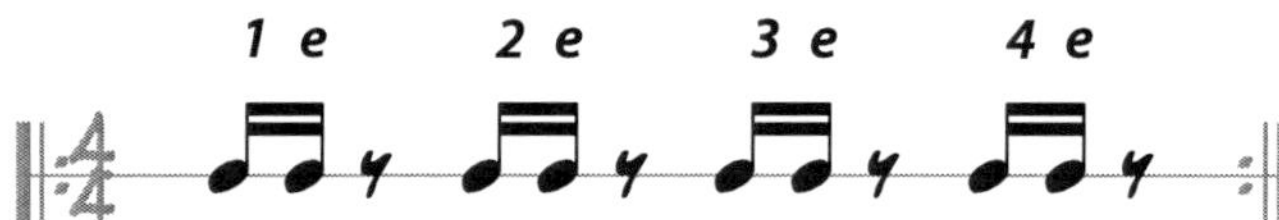

9

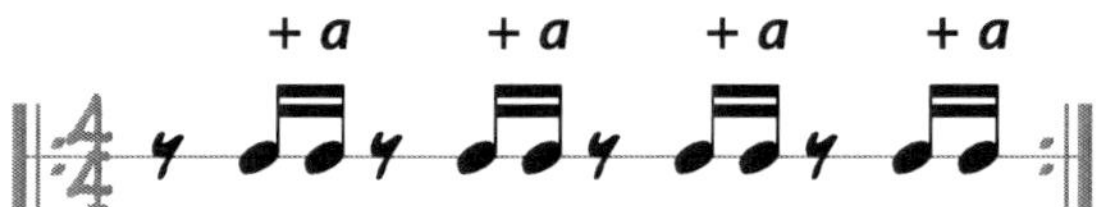

10

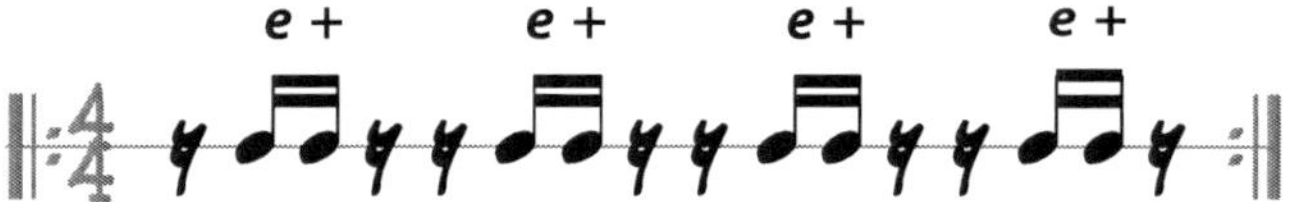

11

e e e e

12

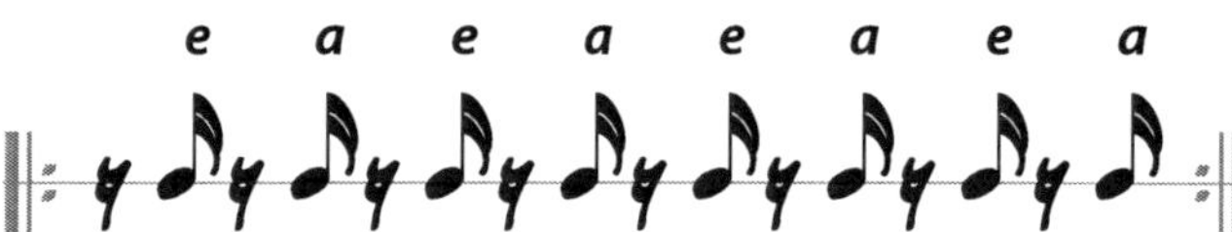

PART 4

SIXTEENTH-NOTE TRIPLET GROOVES

AUDIO TRACKS

♩ =120

1

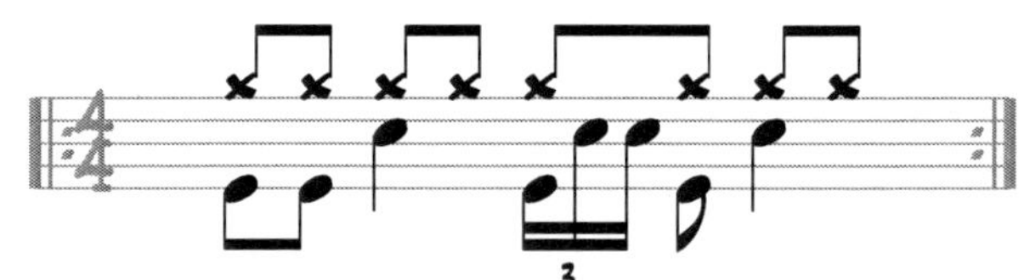

2

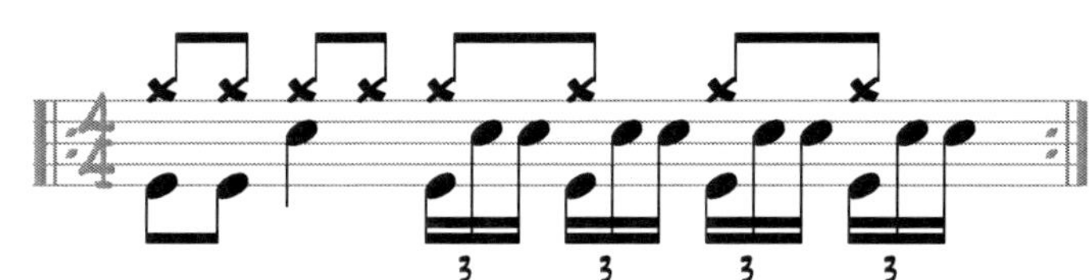

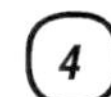

3

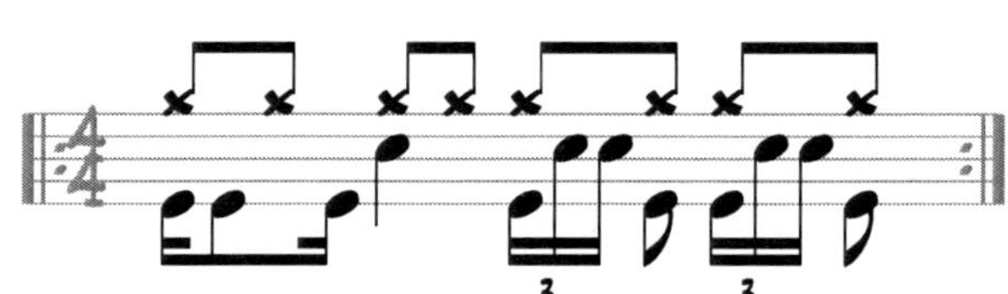

4

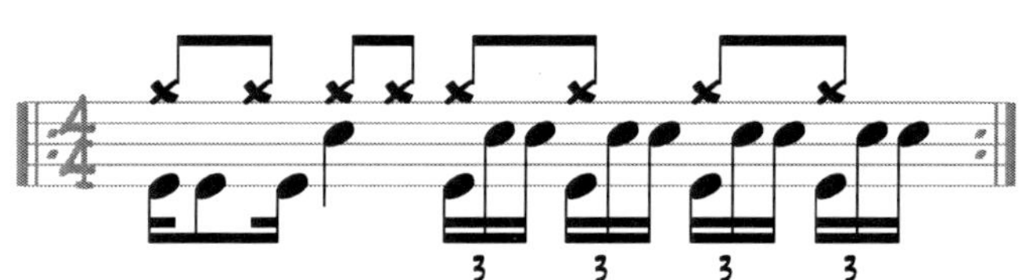

5

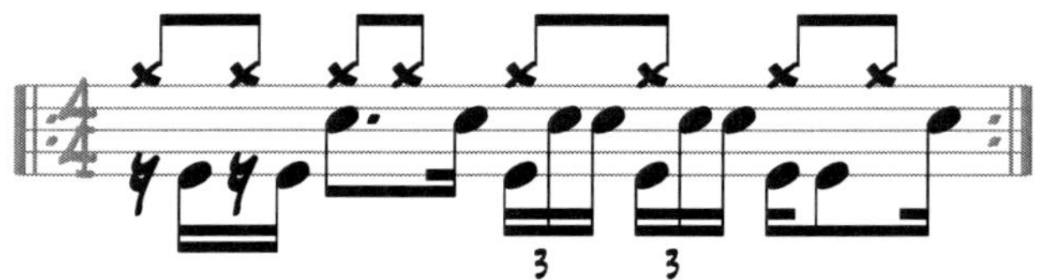

6

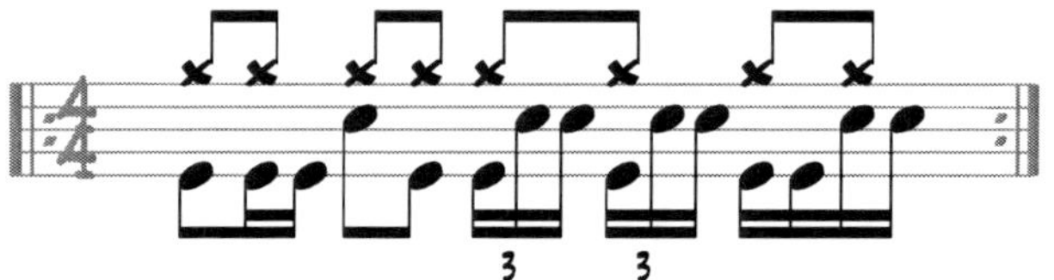

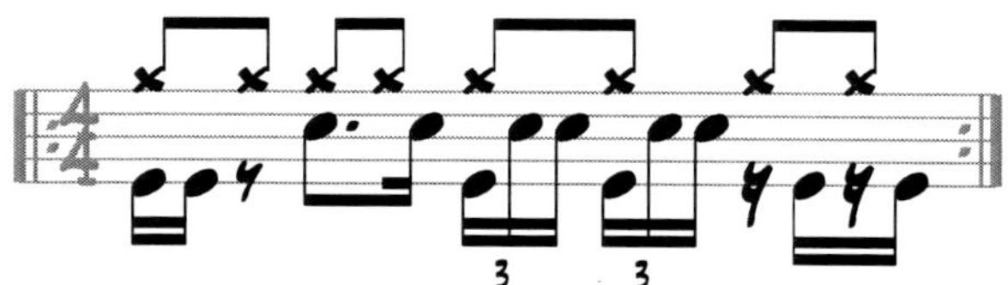

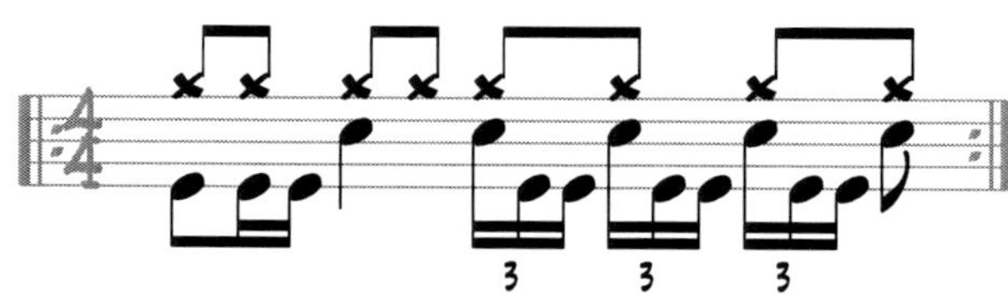

9

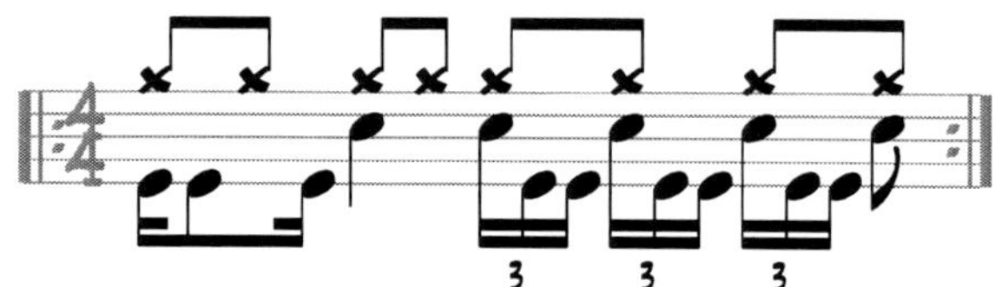

10

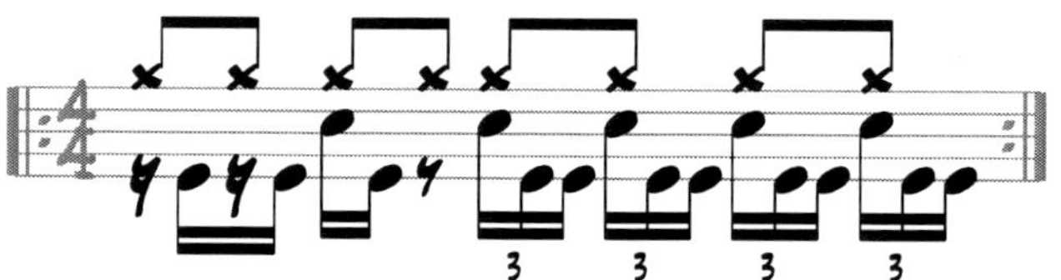

11

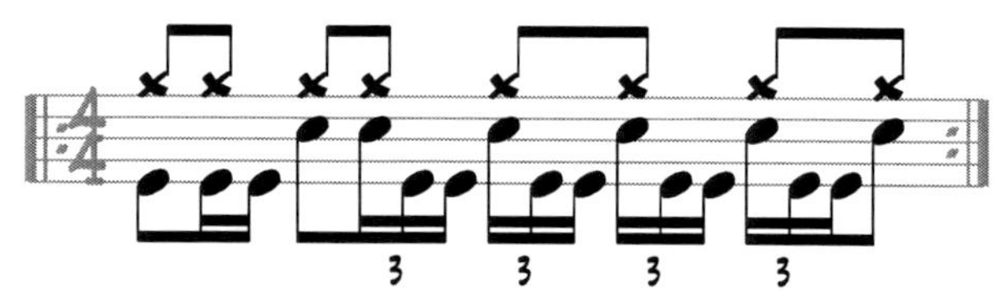

12

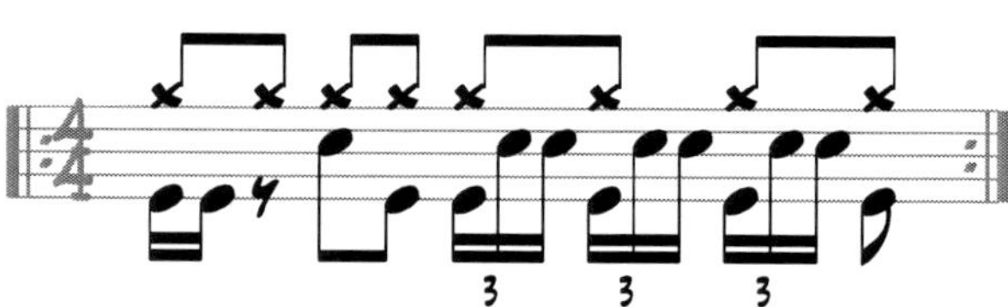

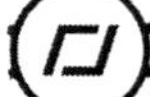

(13)

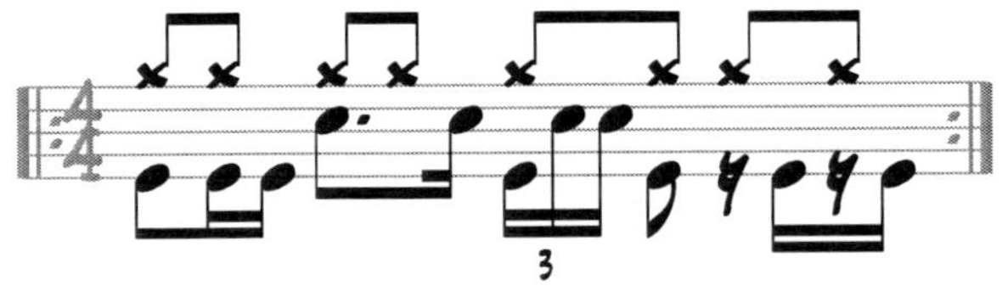

(14)

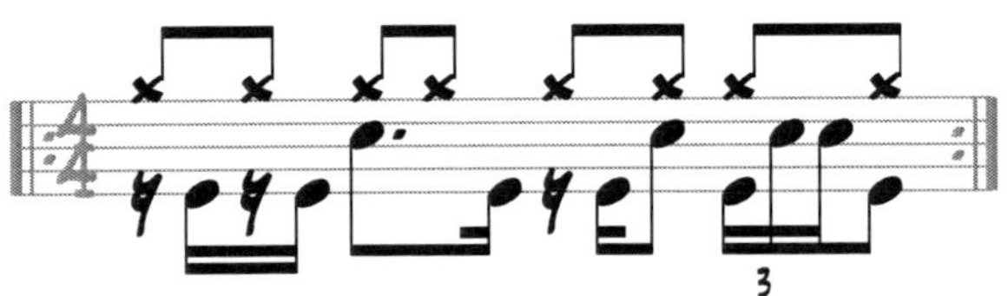

(15)

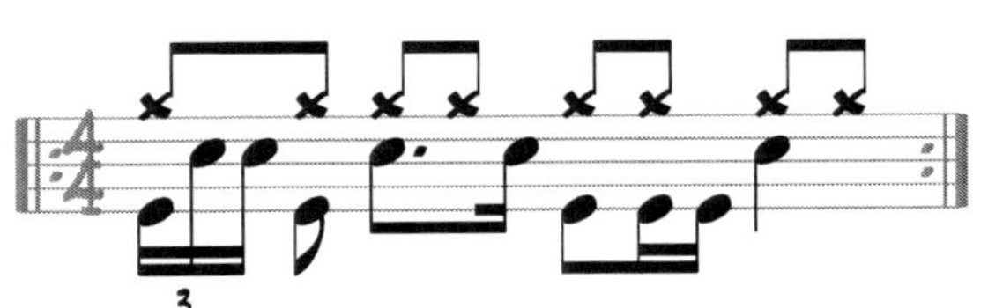

(16)

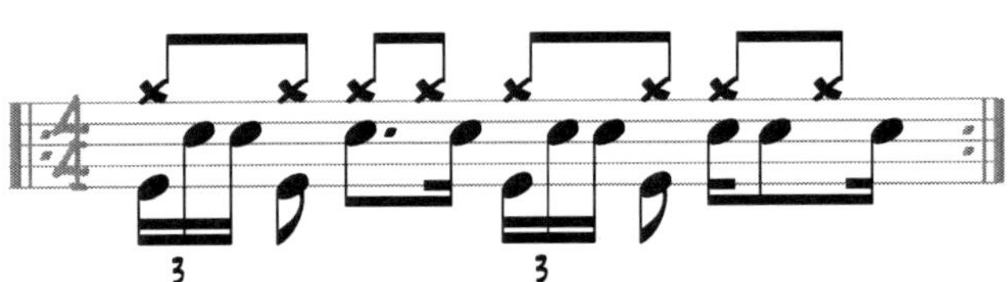

(17)

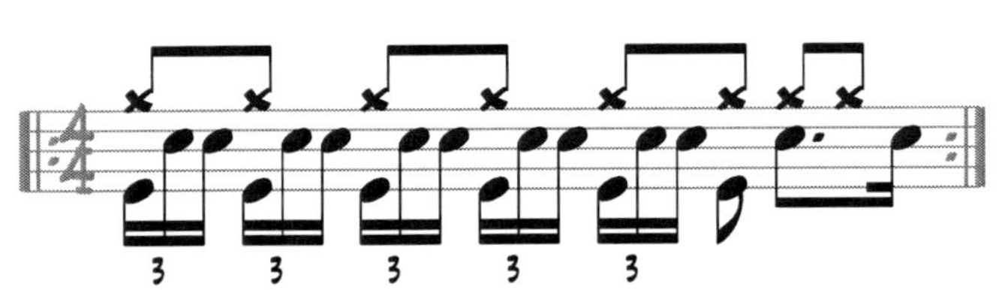

(18)

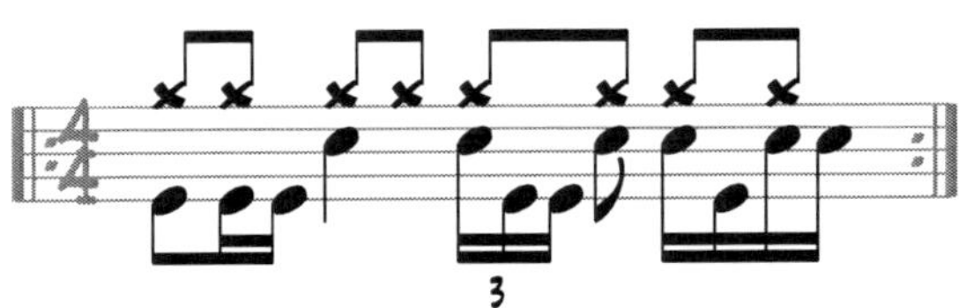

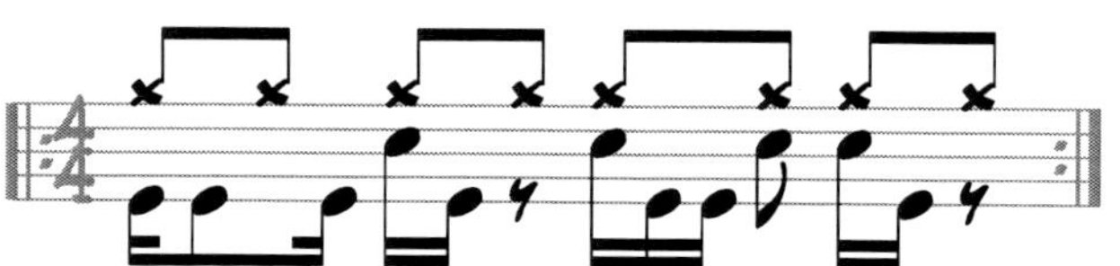

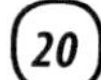

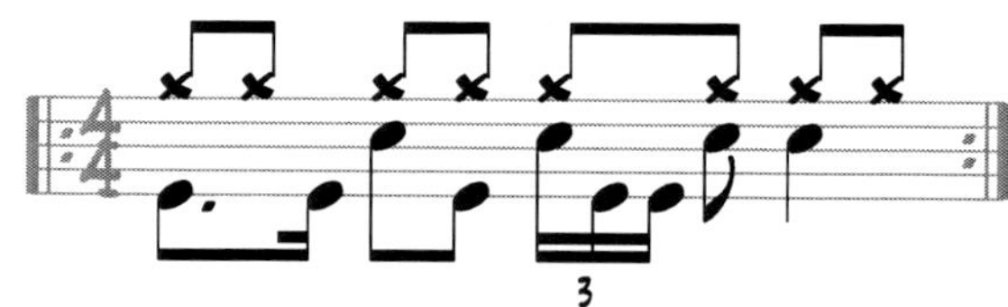

21

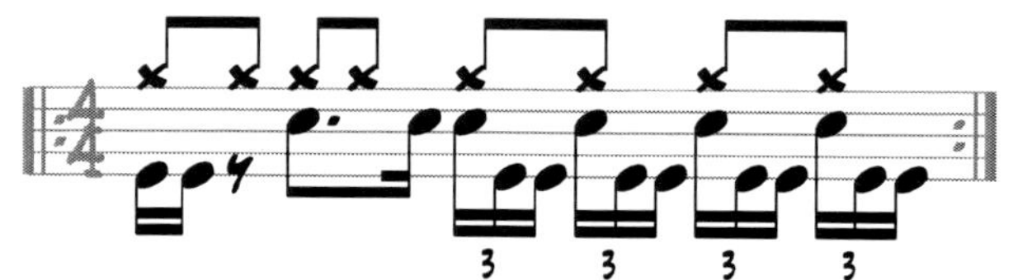

22

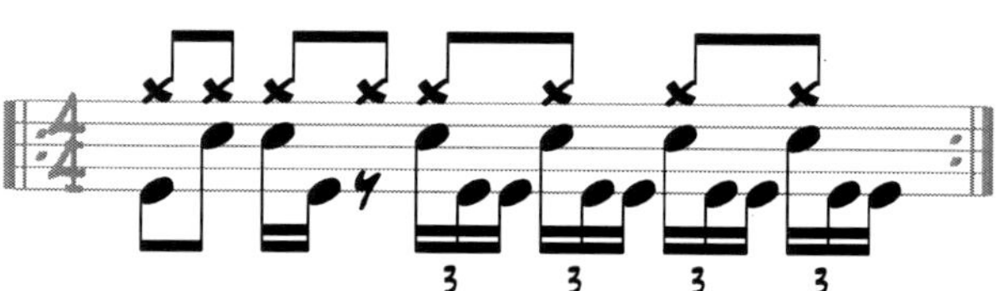

23

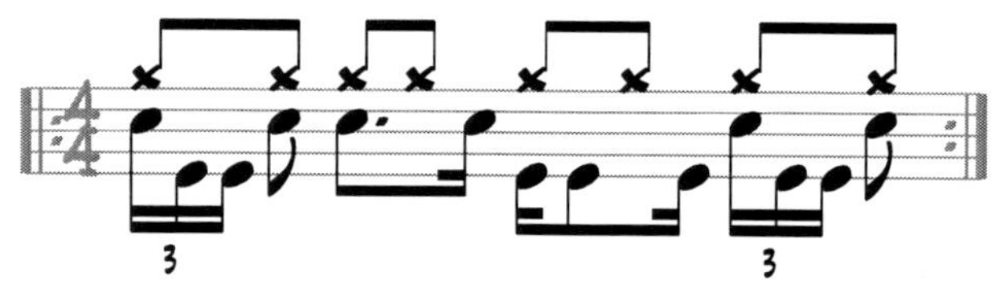

24

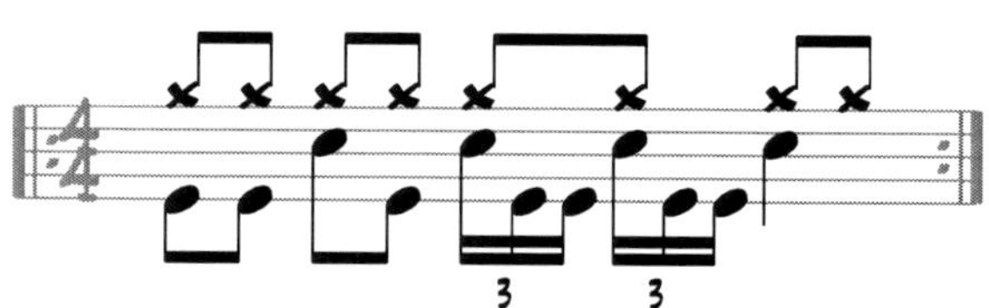

25

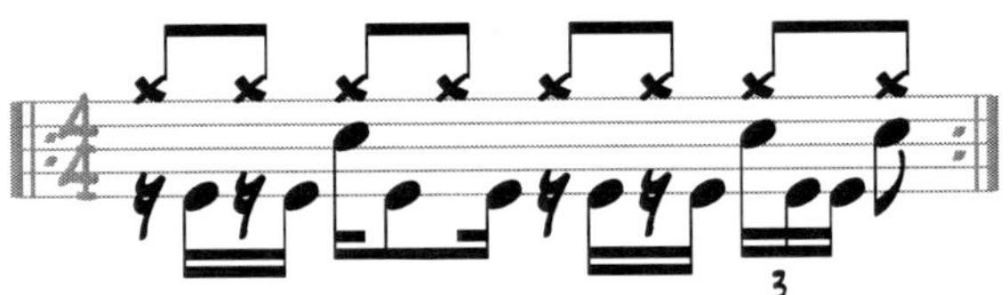

26

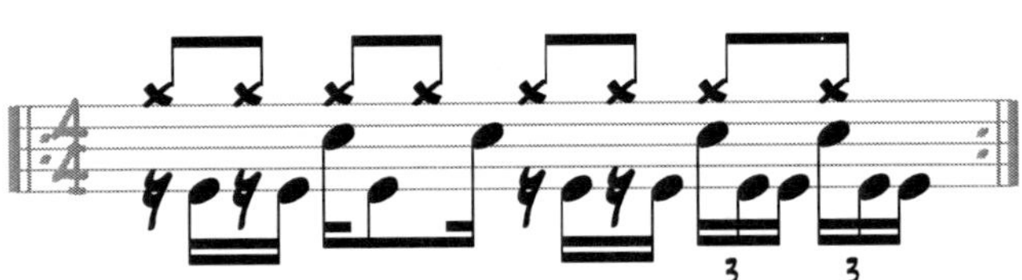

27

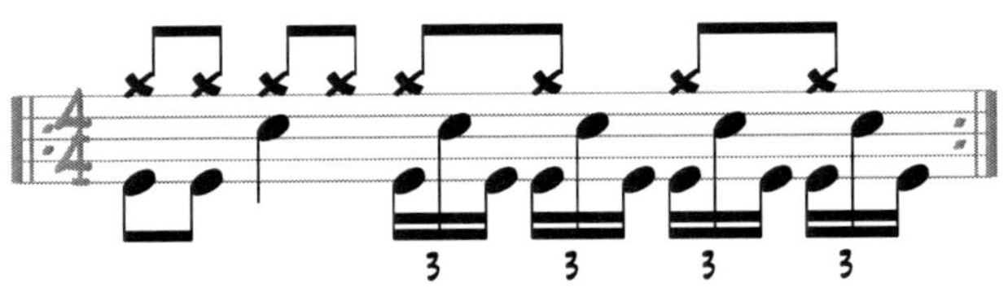

28

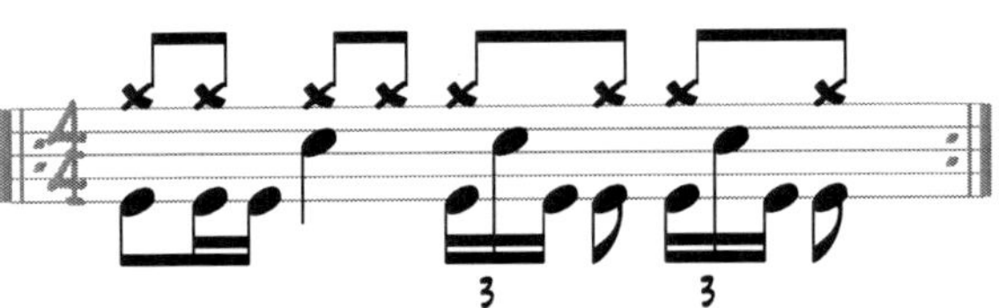

29

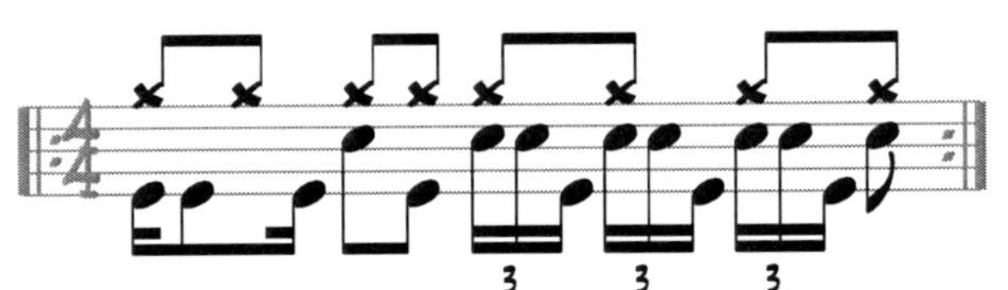

30

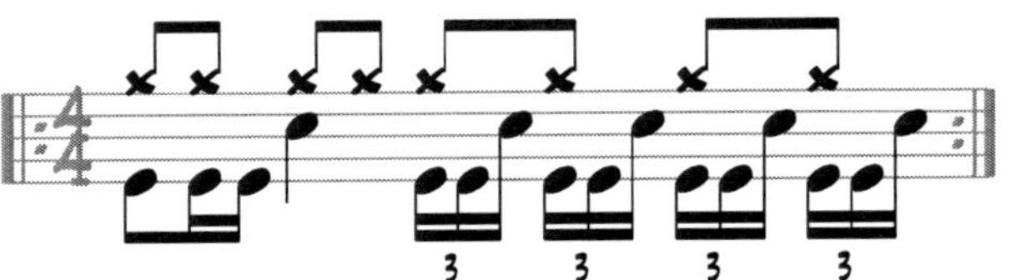

PART 5

TRIPLET-FEEL GROOVES

AUDIO TRACKS

5. TRIPLET-FEEL GROOVES

PART 5

♩ =120

1

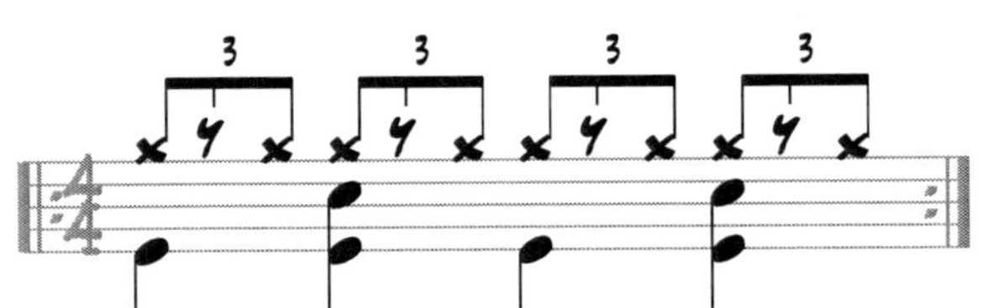

2

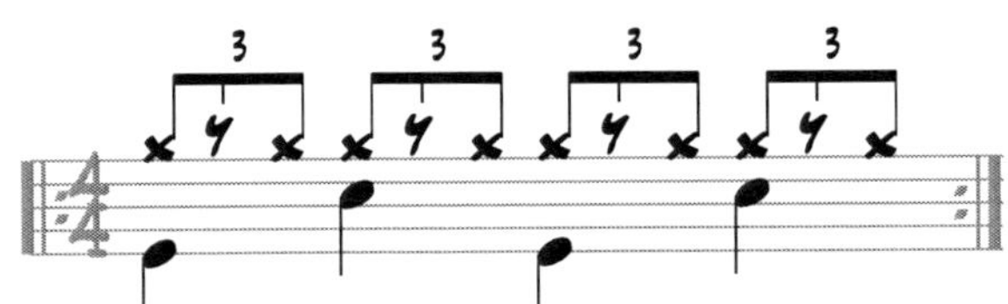

3

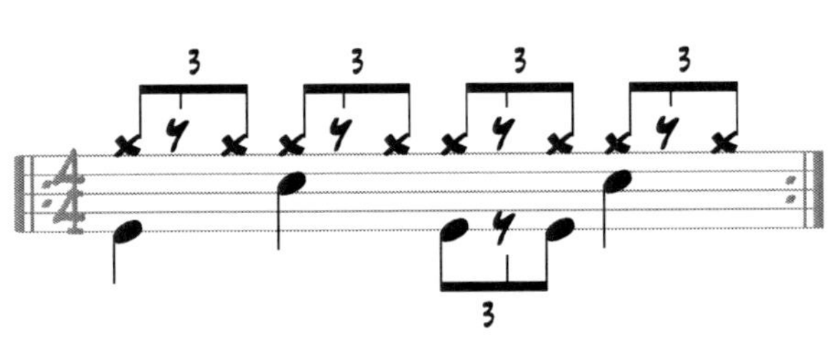

4

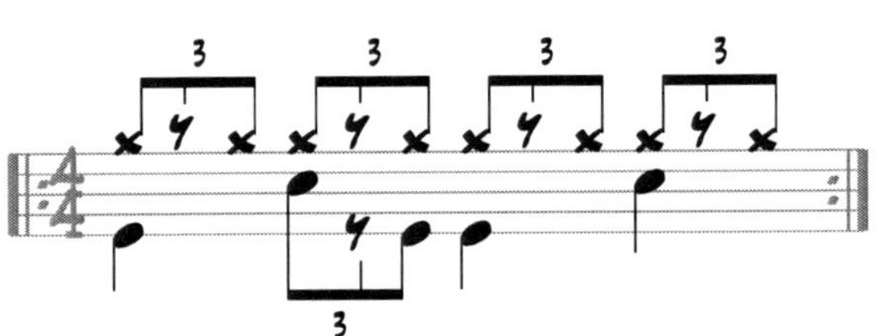

5

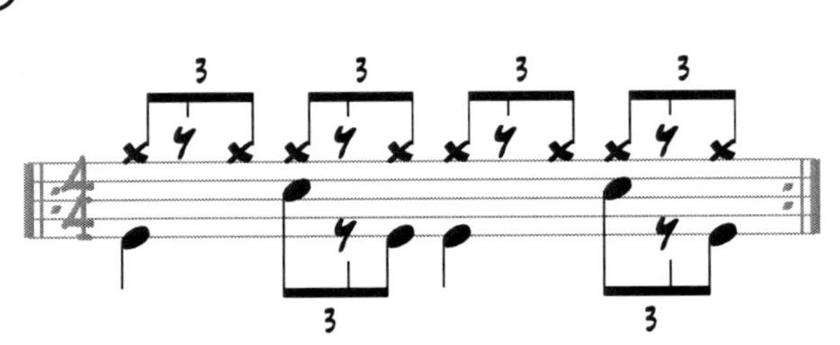

6

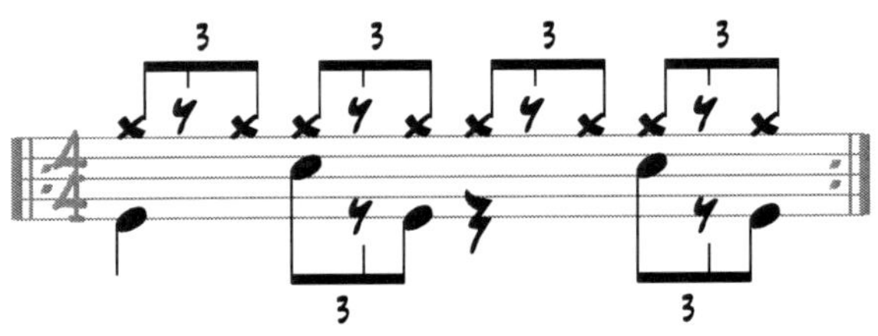

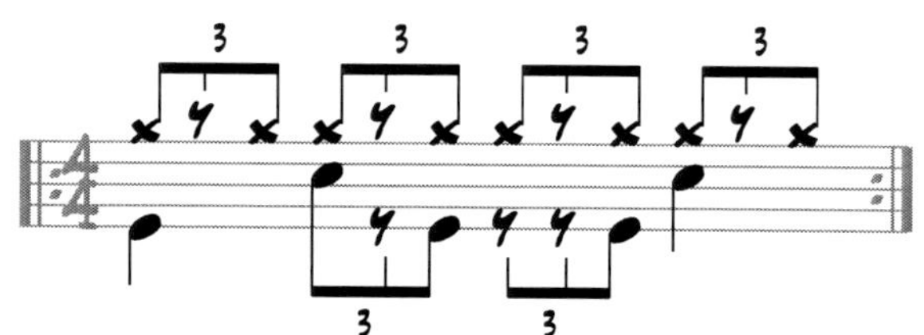

8

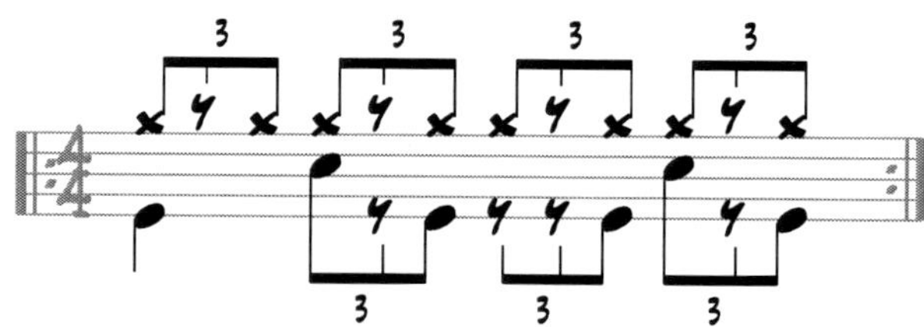

9

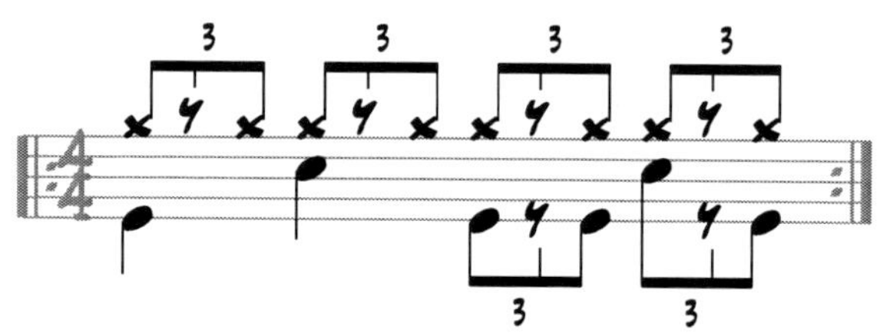

10

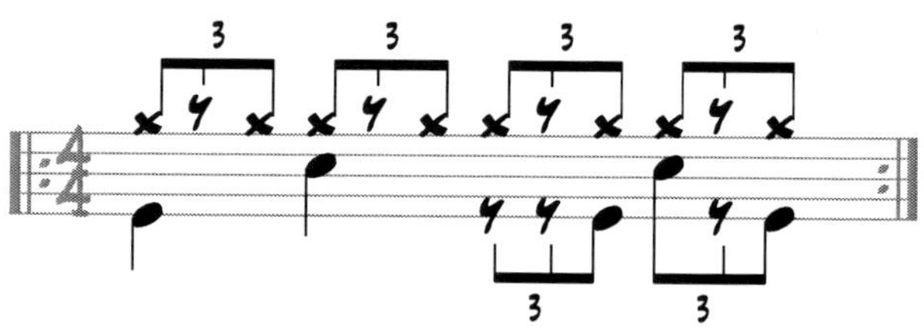

11

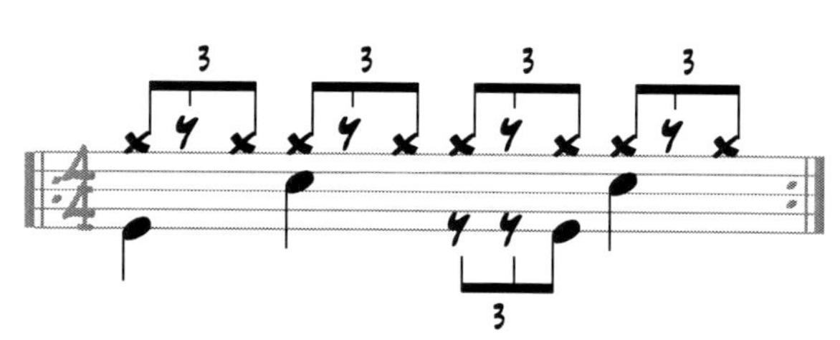

12

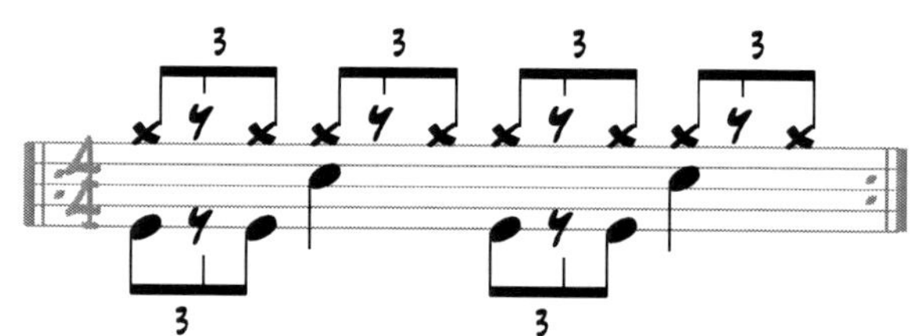

13

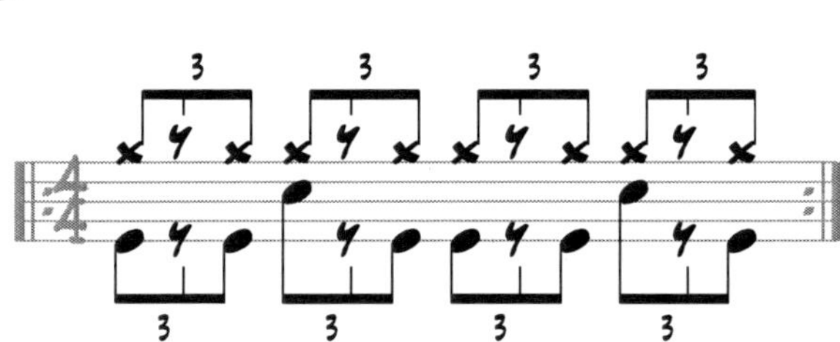

14

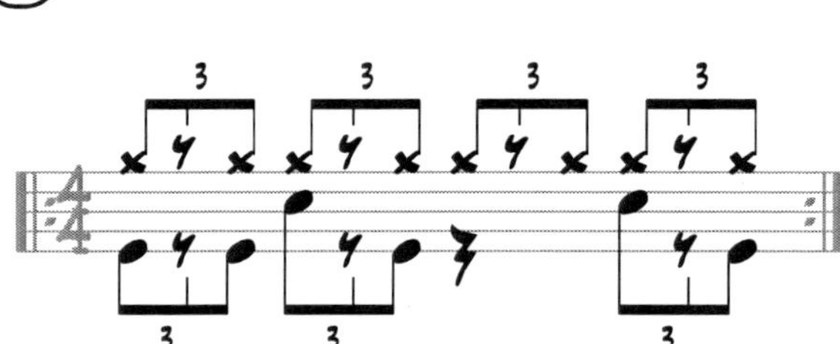

15

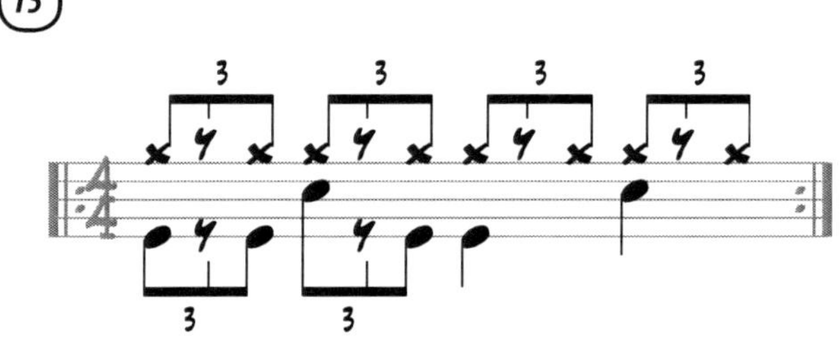

16

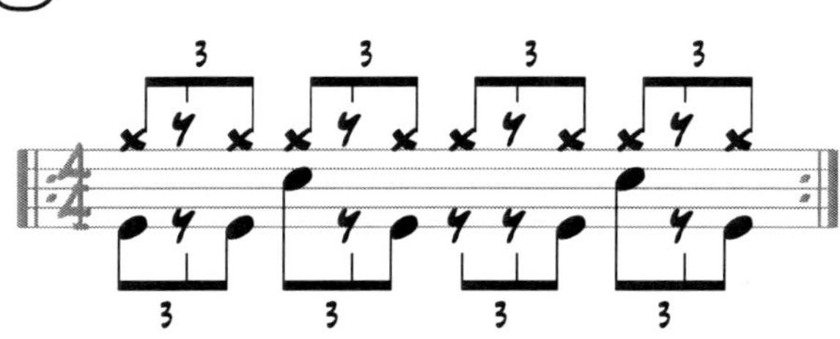

17

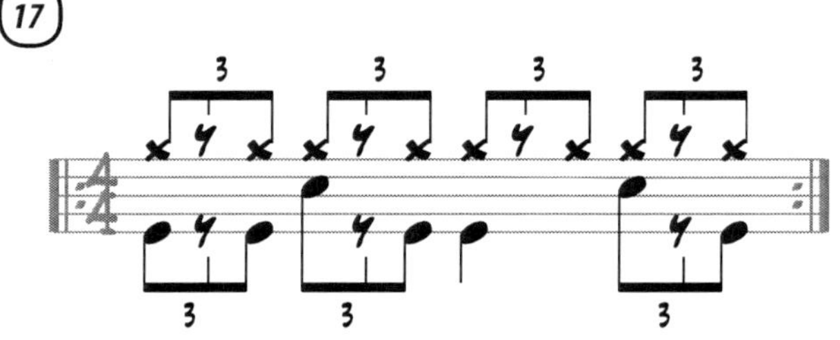

18

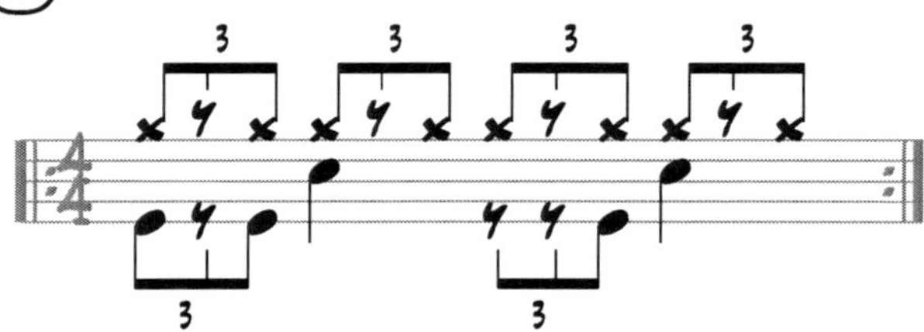

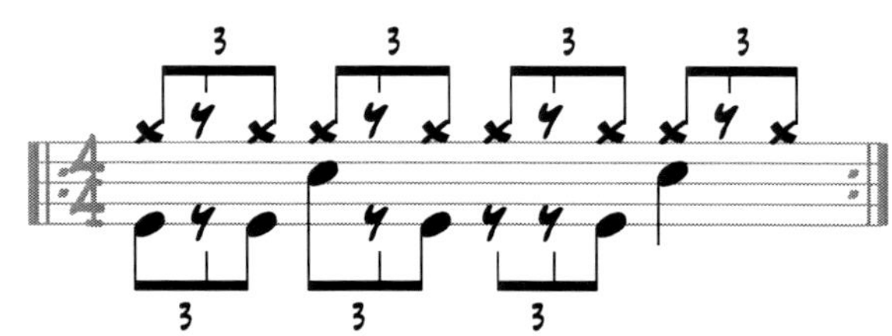

20

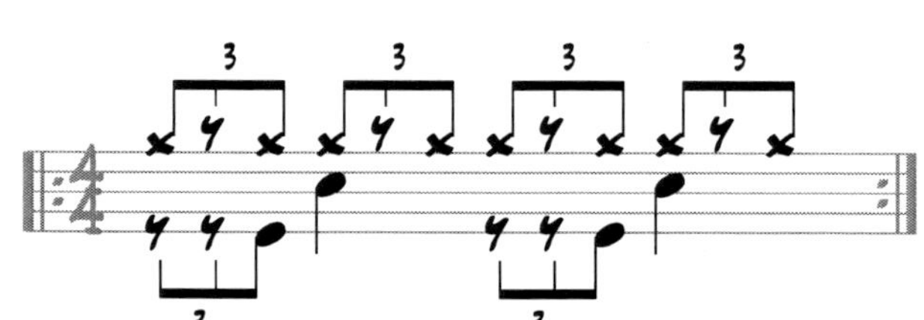

21

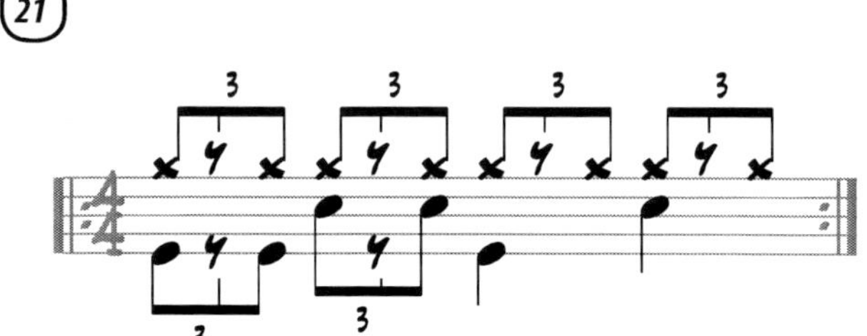

22

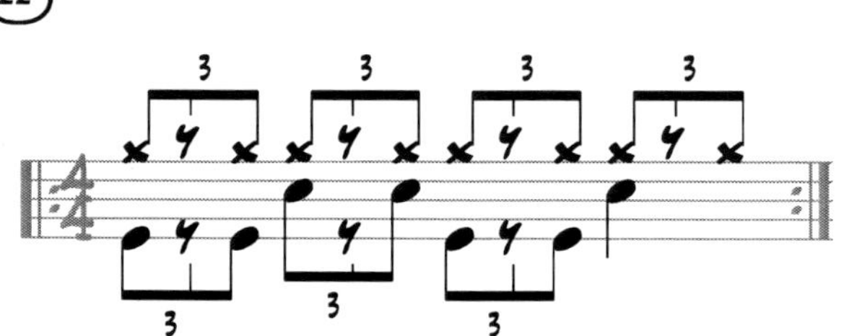

23

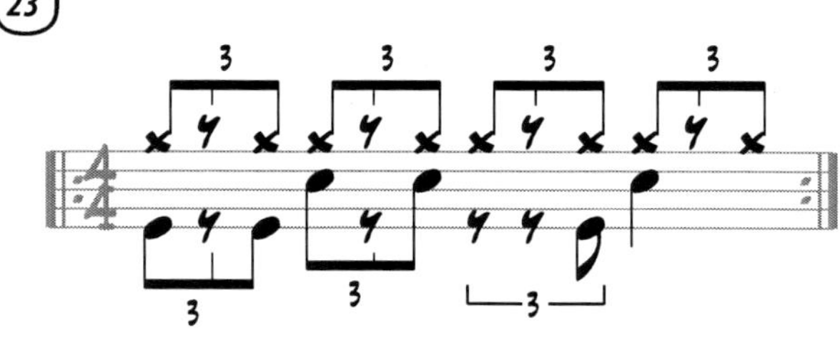

24

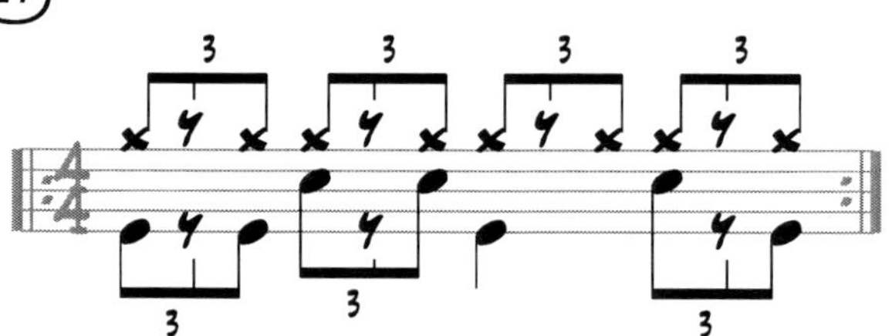

25

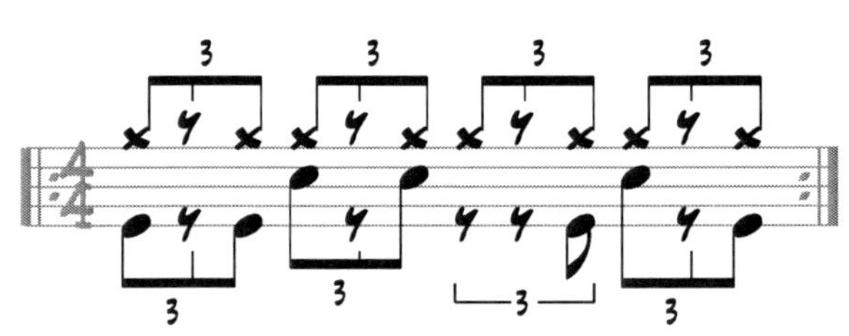

26

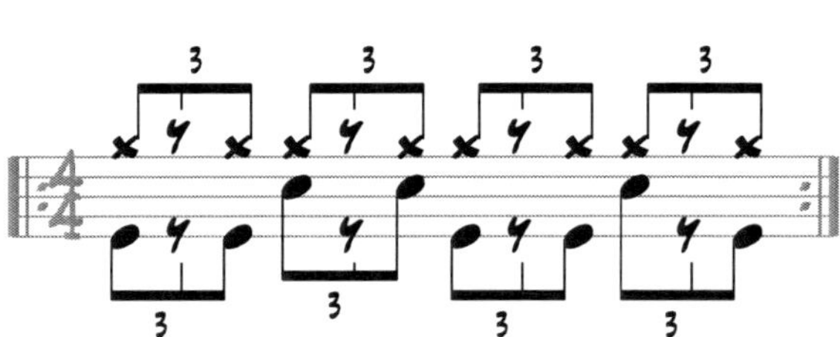

27

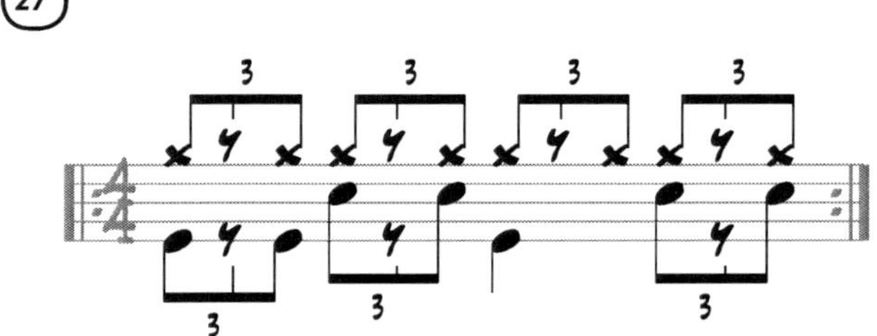

28

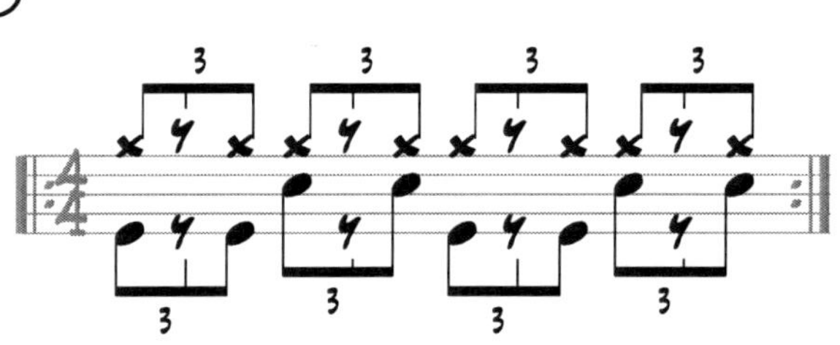

29

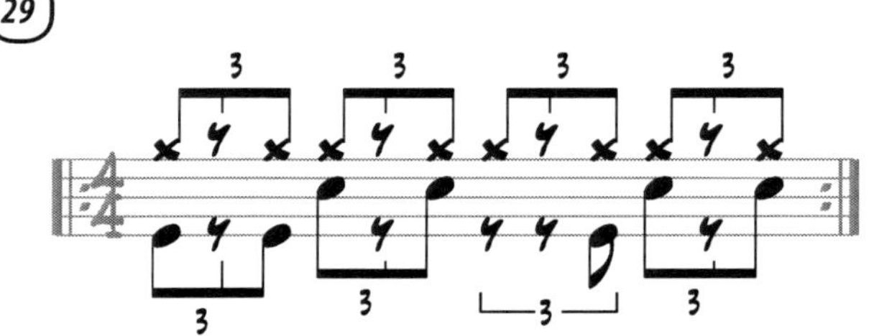

30

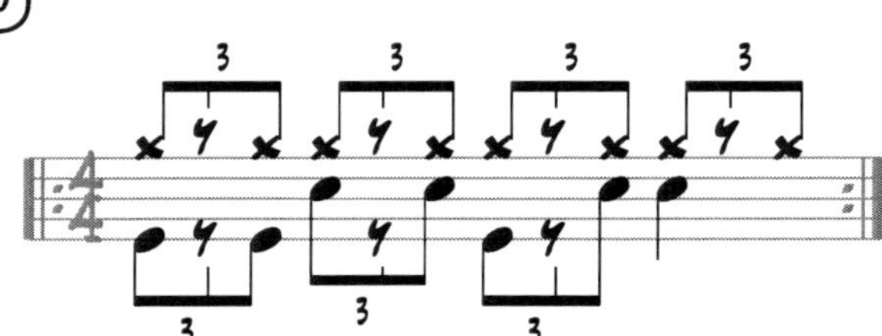

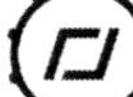

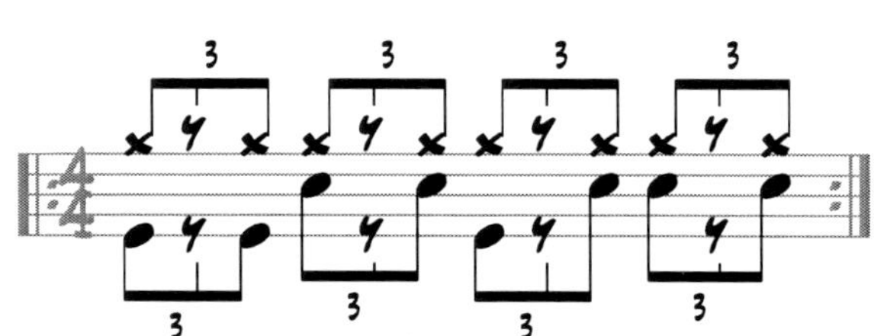

32

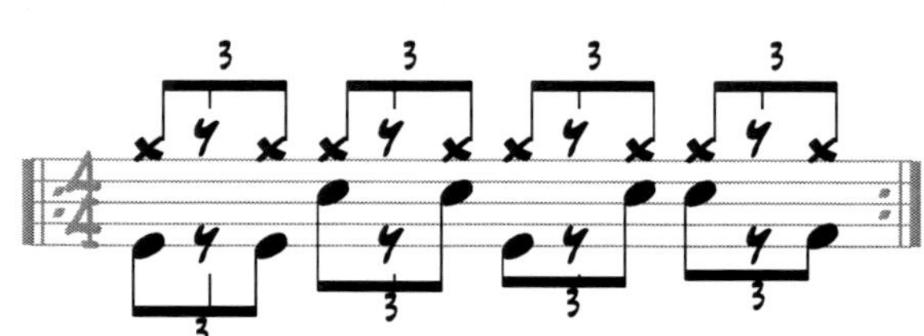

33

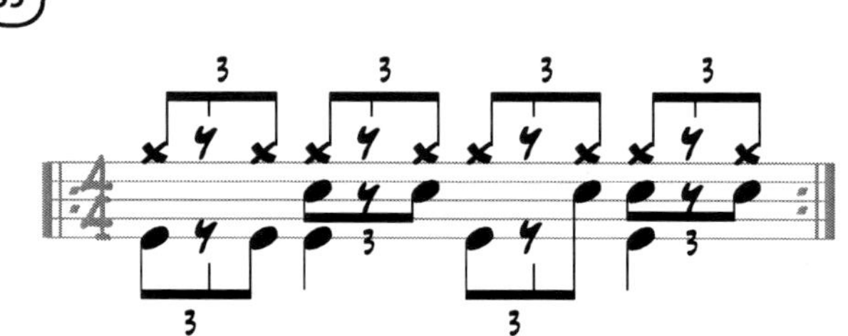

34

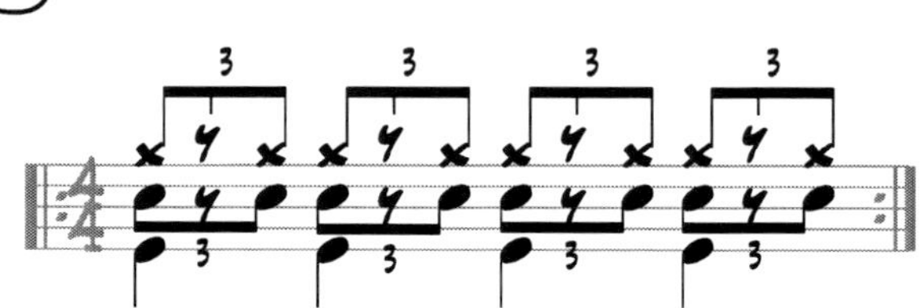

35

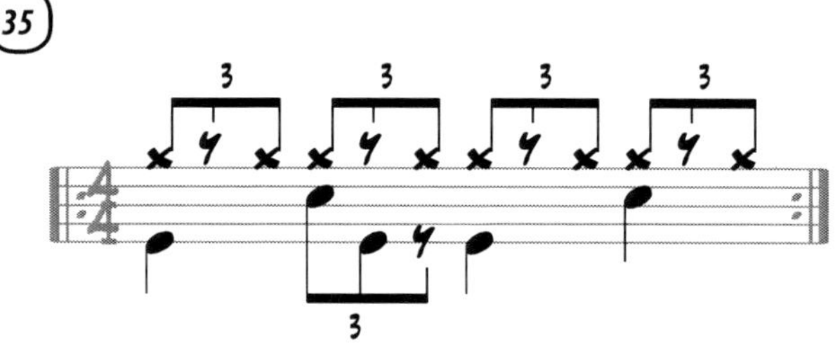

36

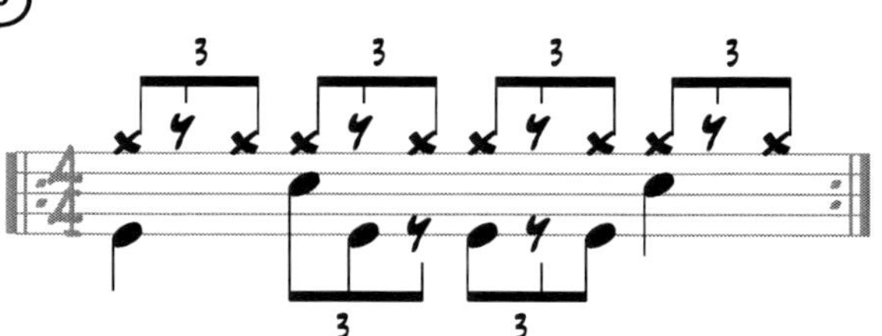

37

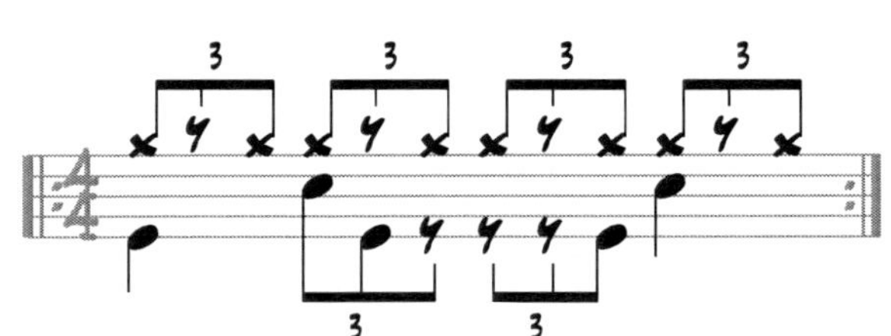

38

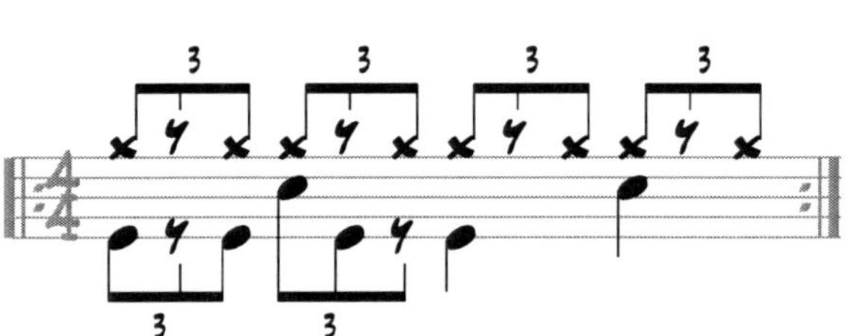

39

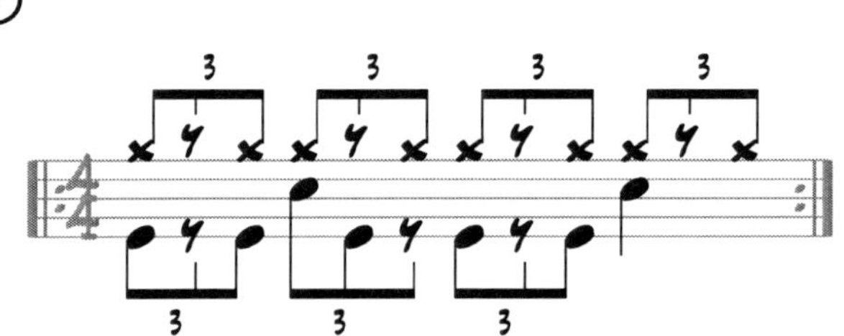

40

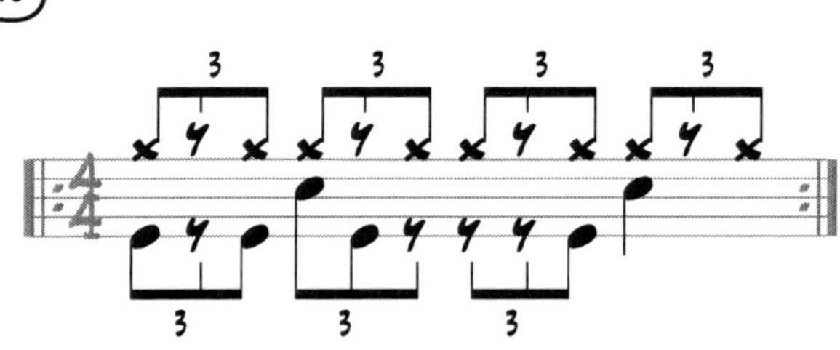

Other Mel Bay Percussion Books

Other Mel Bay Percussion Books

The Rhythm Encyclopedia (Woods)
100 Famous Funk Beats (Payne)
100 Legendary Hip Hop Beats (Prushko)
100 Legendary Modern Rock Drum Beats (Prushko)
100 Legendary Rock Drum Fills (Prushko)
Advanced Rock Drumset (D. Gottlieb)
Aquiles Priester: The PsychOctopus Play Along
Aquiles Priester: Inside My PsychoBook
Aquiles Priester's Top 100 Drum Fills DVD
Block Rockin' Beats (Richardson)
Building Blocks of Rock (Richardson)
Complete Funk Drumming Book (Payne)
Drummer's Cookbook (Pickering)
Drummer's Cookbook Volume 2 (Pickering)
Funk Drumming (Payne)
Funky Beats & Breaks for Drumset (Briggs)
Intermediate Rock Drumset (D. Gottlieb)
Rock Drumming & Soloing Methods (Leytham)
Rock Studies for Drumset (Morton)
The Great Drummers of R&B, Funk & Soul (Payne)
Advanced Jazz Drumset (D. Gottlieb)
Inside the Big Band Drum Chart (Fidyk)
Intermediate Jazz Drumset (D. Gottlieb)
Introduction to Swing-Style Drumming (Maroni)
Essential Jazz Percussion (D. Gottlieb/M. Green)
Fusion Drum Styles (Morton)
Jazz & Blues Drumming (Leytham)
Jazz Drum Set Independence (Fidyk)
Fundamentals of Rhythm for the Drummer (Maroni)
Jazz Drumset Basics (D. Gottlieb)
Jazz Time Part One: The Basics (Briggs)
Studio/Jazz Drum Cookbook (Pickering)
Rock Drumset Basics (D. Gottlieb)
Kid's Rock Drum Method (Richardson)
Beginning Rock Drum Chart (Richardson)
Rudimental Drumset Solos for the Musical Drummer (Leytham)

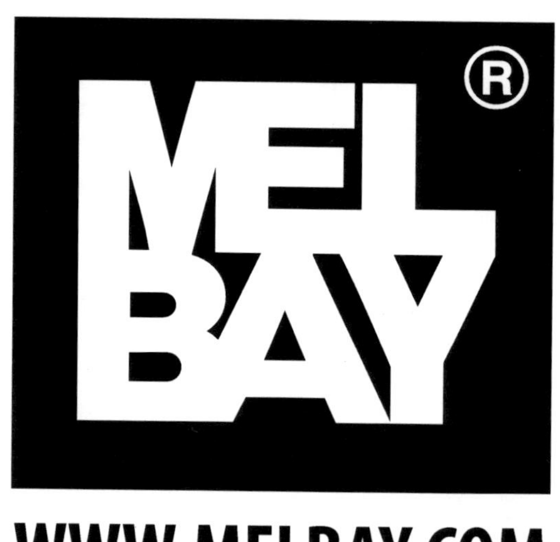

WWW.MELBAY.COM